In the Shadow
of Plenty

George Grant

Christian Liberty Press

Arlington Heights, Illinois

Library of Congress Catalog Card Number 86–050794
ISBN 0–930462–17–3

Printed by
Christian Liberty Press
502 West Euclid Avenue
Arlington Heights, Illinois 60004

Unless otherwise noted, all Scripture quotations are from the New King James Version of the Bible, copyrighted in 1984 by Thomas Nelson, Inc., Nashville, Tennessee.

Cover design by Chris Kou
Layout by Edward J. Shewan

Printed in the United States of America

TABLE OF CONTENTS

PART I THE BIBLICAL BLUEPRINT: 10 PRINCIPLES

PART II THE BIBLICAL BLUEPRINT: 3 STRATEGIES

ACKNOWLEDGMENTS

In his renowned *Memoirs* Sir James Mackintosh, the eighteenth century's "philosophical politician" wrote a noble tribute to his devoted wife. In acknowledging the efforts of my beloved Karen, I can do little better than to rephrase his sentiments, his divine union being so akin to my own.

"I was guided in my choice only by the blind affection of my youth. I found an intelligent companion and a tender friend, a prudent monitress, the most faithful of wives, and a mother as tender as children ever had the fortune to have. I met a woman who by the tender management of my weaknesses, has painlessly taken to correcting the most pernicious of them.... During the most critical periods of my life, she has preserved order in my affairs, from the care of which she relieved me. She has gently reclaimed me from depression; she has propped my weak and irresolute nature; and she has been perpetually at hand to admonish my heedlessness and improvidence. To her I owe whatever I am; to her whatever I shall be."

Others, who have stood in the gap as I have labored to "tangibilitate" this manuscript include: my elders Frank Marshall, Kemper Crabb, Dave Marshall, and Brian Martin; my mentors James B. Jordan, David Chilton, and Gary North; my publishers David Dunham and John Mauldin; my HELP co-workers J. D. McWilliams and Suzanne Martin; my midnight oil compatriots G. K. Chesterton, Lloyd Billingsley, William Gibson, Bruce Sterling, Alexander Schmemann, R. L. Dabney, R. J. Rushdoony, J. R. R. Tolkien, and (believe it if you can, Captain) William Ashbless; and of course my dearest friends in life: Ponch, Peut, and Punk.

The Second Sunday of Epiphany, 1986 Humble, Texas

FOREWORD

By Herbert Schlossberg, Ph.D.,
Author of *Idols for Destruction and The Fragrance of Persecution*

In the seventies, eighties, and nineties, there has grown to great intensity a debate within the evangelical world concerning the relative importance of evangelism and social action, the latter of which was understood principally as the helping of the poor. For most of those in the fray on both sides, evangelism meant the preaching of the Gospel to bring people to a saving faith in Christ. The social action side carried a meaning that was somewhat more vague—for some, it meant personal charitable activity; for others, it meant primarily supporting humanitarian activity by the State.

This debate was evidence of a terrible weakness in the church, in both its theology and its practice. Evangelicals were united in their insistence on the Bible as the rule of faith and practice, and yet were unable to realize that the debate was being conducted on grounds that were foreign to Biblical thinking. The Law, the Prophets, the Gospels, and the Epistles are devoid of any idea that there is a contradiction between the communication of God's grace on the one hand and the doing of good works on the other. Indeed, it was in the midst of his missionary journeys that Paul organized the collection of funds for the Christians in Jerusalem who were living in privation. That ministry was the prime example of the unity between believing rightly and doing good.

Throughout the New Testament, love is described as the identifying mark of the Christian community to its pagan neighbors, its authenticating feature, that which proves that God's life is in its midst. James's statement that "faith without works is dead" is of one piece with the entire Biblical witness that the separation of the inner life from the exterior one makes no sense. Similarly, works without faith is of no religious significance except as a continuing testimony of the futility of trying to save ourselves. The task remains for each generation of Christians to ascertain how it can live an integrated life, fully exemplifying the inner and outer dimensions in the wholeness that only Biblical faith makes possible.

Once this is agreed upon, we're ready to address the thorniest issue of those debates: whether our responsibilities to the poor are to be discharged primarily by personal charitable action or through supporting the humanitarian policies of the State. There may have been some excuse to debate that issue ten years ago, but there is none today. Now that the "War on poverty" has entered its third decade, its record of abysmal failure is becoming increasingly clear. The substitution by officers of the state of humanitarian "good works" for Christian charity has been a disaster almost without precedent.

We now have presented for us in bone-chilling detail by such writers as P. T. Bauer, George Gilder, Marvin Olasky, and Charles Murray how poor people, in our own country and abroad, have been transformed by humanitarian policy into helpless wards of the State, completely dehumanized by the programs that were supposed to be motivated by compassion. The most bitter denunciations of the State welfare system come from the pens of black economists Thomas Sowell, Glen Lowrie, and Walter Williams, fed up with seeing their people destroyed by the policies of "compassion."

It's a shame that we have to keep on going over that ground to convince people that State welfare is not the means for being obedient to the Biblical commands to help the poor. Yet, the battle has been largely won on the intellectual front, and we have only a mopping up operation to conduct, as well as the political task of making that victory operational.

But something is missing. If the welfare system is the wrong method for helping the poor, are we sure we want to find the right method? The political left has not been bashful about ascribing opposition to welfare to a callous disregard for the well-being of the poor. There may be something self-serving in that ascription, but there is also some truth in it. A friend of mine, who headed up one of the Reagan administration's poverty agencies, recently told me of his experiences after taking over the agency from the preceding administration. He found that the political left fought him every step of the way, as he expected. But he also discovered that conservatives opposed him in his quest to see that the legitimate cause of justice for the poor was served. He concluded that many conservatives are not interested in the poor.

Christians should not be in the position of choosing between those opposing pagan ideals. The State is not our savior and we do not look to it for earthly redemption, nor is it the conduit through which we advance our own interests at the expense of our fellow citizens.

That brings us to the questions of how Christians are to obey the Biblical mandate to serve the poor after they have identified the State welfare system for what it is. How can we recognize who we are to help and who we are to avoid helping? How can we accomplish the task through the communal actors and activities that the Biblical commands place at the center of our loyalties: family and Church? How can we ensure that poor people become productive and join us in assisting the helpless, rather than becoming our wards and dependents? How can we translate the prescriptions that worked in pastoral settings three thousand years ago into terms that make them effective in doing God's work in the twenty-first century? Above all, how can we comprehend our responsibility to help the poor in such a way that it is integrated with a Biblical understanding of the lordship of Christ over the whole cosmos, so that we don't isolate this work from the rest of life, thus idolizing it and turning it into something evil?

We're indebted to George Grant for helping us see our way through this complex of issues. Rather than continuing to beat the dead carcass of the welfare system, he leaves the putrefying mess and heads for fresh air. He shows us our real responsibilities, quoting the same Biblical passages as the defenders of public welfare. But he does it without the sense of helplessness and guilt that are the identifying features of humanist preachments, including those erroneously advanced by Christians.

Moreover, he presents the problem to us in its proper historical context. We don't face unprecedented problems; the poor have been with us from the beginning, and the Christian Church has always been doing something about it. C. H. Spurgeon's orphanages in nineteenth-century London were not as famous as his pulpit, but they were as fully a part of his ministry. We're not isolated in either time or space, Dr. Grant shows us, but are part of a community that has given vigorous service to the poor as far back as the ancients and as near as our families and neighbors. The body of Christ is the ministering agent that accomplishes God's commandments, and that includes the ministry to the poor.

But Dr. Grant intends this book to be a manual for service as well as a tool for understanding our true role in helping poor people. We learn in it how to make visible the hidden poor; how to gather and distribute food; how to find lodging for the homeless; how to minister spiritually as we help physically; how to anticipate and protect against legal challenges; how to work together as families and communities, thus avoiding defeat by the insidious atomization that is wreaking so much havoc on the larger society—all within the context of Biblical truth.

I have not read anything else so useful in helping us move away from the necessary but limited task of criticism and toward practical accomplishment in this vital area. Dr. Grant has based his work on solid analysis, solid theology, and solid experience. But it's not the last word. If we're able to put what he has told us into practice, we should be able to build up a solid body of knowledge that will make the next manual that much more useful. This process is called standing on the shoulders of our predecessors. I think Dr. Grant will be happy to have his shoulders stood upon.

PART I
THE BIBLICAL BLUEPRINT:
10 PRINCIPLES

Blessed is he who considers the poor, The Lord will deliver him in the time of trouble. The Lord will preserve him and keep him alive, and he will be blessed on the earth.... The Lord will strengthen him on his bed of illness and sustain him on his sickbed.

Psalm 41:1–3

AUTHOR'S INTRODUCTION

There is starving in the shadow of plenty.

Still.

Poverty abounds in the midst of affluence. And this, despite a massive "war on poverty" that has marshaled billions of dollars, thousands of experts, and hundreds of programs into an unprecedented arsenal of social activism.

Pitiful ragmen haunt the garbage-strewn alleyways just off Michigan Avenue in Chicago.

Ruthless teenage gangs, riven with hunger and hopelessness, pillage the barrios of east L.A.

Young mothers from Gary, Indiana's "burned over district" frequent the infamous "lakeside strip," made over in skintight gold lame and spandex, supplementing welfare with a few "tricks" on the sly.

With their every earthly possession crammed into filthy shopping bags, the homeless women of Manhattan's midtown wander aimlessly through the rush-hour crowds in Grand Central Station.

Tenement dwellers in east St. Louis line up in swollen fury outside dilapidated government buildings after their food stamps allotment fails to suffice to the end of the month.

In a tent city hugging the bank of the San Jacinto River just north of Houston's vast petrochemical complex, elementary school children disembark from their buses and trudge slowly through the muck and the mire toward the cardboard shanties they call "home."

The "war on poverty" was supposed to rid our land of the horrid specter of hunger and privation. It was supposed to fit every citizen for productivity and self-sufficiency. It was supposed to usher in a new era of abundance and prosperity. According to its champion, President Lyndon Johnson, it was supposed "to eliminate the paradox of poverty in the midst of plenty."

But more than three decades later, the paradox remains. The "war on poverty" is a dismal failure. Even more recent Presidents like Bill Clinton have had to admit that big government welfare programs have created a permanent underclass of hopeless Americans.

Poverty is actually increasing. In 1950, one-in-twelve Americans (about 21 million) lived below the poverty line. In 1979, that figure had risen to one-in-nine (about 26 million). Today, one-in-seven (36.5 million) fall below the line.

More than twenty percent of all American children live in poverty (up from 9.3% in 1950 and 14.9% in 1970). And for black children under age six, the figures are even more dismal: a record 51.2%.

Today, 24.3% percent of elderly women living alone live in poverty, all too often in abject poverty, up from a mere 7% in 1954.

As many as three million Americans are homeless, living out of the backs of their cars, under bridges, in abandoned warehouses, atop street side heating grates, or in lice-infested public shelters. Even at the height of the depression, when dust-bowl refugees met with the "grapes of wrath" on America's highways and byways, there have never been so many dispossessed wanderers.

Crime is up. Educational standards are down. Unemployment figures have finally climbed down from "recession" highs to "recovery" lows, but before the bureaucrats strike up the band, close scrutiny should be given to the fact that long-term and hard-core unemployment continues unabated.

Amidst all this human carnage, where have the masterminds behind the "war on poverty" been? What have they been doing?

Very simply, they have been squandering vast amounts of time, money, and resources.

In 1951, spending for all the government's social welfare programs barely topped $4 billion. By 1976, the "Great Society" had far superseded the legacy of "Camelot," spending $34.6 billion. In 1981, welfare activists were appalled by the "Scrooge" sentiment in Washington when social welfare spending was "limited" to a "mere" $316.6 billion! The figure for 1997 topped one trillion dollars!

Food stamps spending rose from $577 million in 1970 to an astonishing high of $26 billion in 1995.

In the two and a half decades since the Eisenhower administration vacated the White House, since the "war on poverty" was initiated: health and medical expenditures have increased sixfold (in constant dollars); public assistance costs have risen *thirteenfold* (again in constant dollars); education expenditures outstripped pre-reform levels *twenty-four times;* social insurance costs rose *twenty-seven times;* and housing costs inflated a whopping *one hundred twenty-nine times.*

By 1996, social welfare spending of every sort, including social security, Aid for Families with Dependent Children (AFDC), Unemployment Insurance, Supplemental Security Income (SSI), Workman's Compensation, and Food Stamps claimed 52.7% of the federal budget.

But instead of making things better, this extremely costly, ever-escalating "war on poverty" has only made things worse. The very policies that were intended to *help* the poor have only aggravated their problems. Welfare policies have undermined families, encouraged promiscuity, promoted dependence, and provided disincentives to work and industry.

The "war on poverty" has been fought with righteous verve and passionate zeal. But what are the spoils of this "war"?

There is more misery than ever before.

There is more hopelessness than ever before.

There is more poverty than ever before.

Why?

Why have all the best-laid plans fallen to ruin? Why have all the grandest of resources been so blatantly squandered? Why has the "war" been an utter failure?

Why? Because the "war on poverty" completely ignored, and as a consequence violated, God's blueprint for living: the Bible.

The bureaucrats in Washington who have waged the "war on poverty" over the years certainly cannot be faulted for their concern over the plight of the poor (Psalm 41:1). Where they went wrong was in taking matters into their own hands. Instead of adhering to the wise and inerrant counsel of scripture, they "did what was right in their own eyes" (Judges 21:25). For all their good intentions, their programs were blatantly man centered. In other words, they were humanistic!

"All Scripture is given by inspiration of God, and is profitable for doctrine, for reproof, for correction, for instruction in righteousness, that the man of God may be complete, thoroughly equipped for every good work." (2 Timothy 3:16–17). Thus, to attempt the "good work" of poverty relief without taking heed to the clear instructions of the Bible is utter foolishness (Romans 1:18–23). It is to invite inadequacy and incompetency (Deuteronomy 28:15). All such attempts are doomed to frustration and failure, as the "war on poverty" has so amply and aptly proven. Humanism and its various programs, policies, and agendas can't work, because humanism is out of touch with reality (Ephesians 5:6). It is fraught with fantasy (Colossians 2:8). Only the Bible can tell us of things as they really are (Psalm 19:7–11). Only the Bible faces reality squarely, practically, completely, and honestly (Deuteronomy 30:11–14). Thus, only the Bible can illumine genuine solutions to the problems that plague mankind (Psalm 119:105).

This book's primary intention is to look simply and briefly at what the Bible says about poverty relief. What does Scripture teach concerning welfare? Or work? Or charity? Or entitlement programs? What about the civil government's role? Or that of private initiative? Or the churches? And what about income redistribution? What does the Bible really say about justice, mercy, and compassion? Or civil rights and affirmative action? Or oppression and bondage?

Once a clear and principled picture has been drawn of the Bible's blueprint for relief, then—and only then—can specific policy recommendations be made (Deuteronomy 15:4–8). Only then can strategies be outlined, tactics designed, and programs initiated (Joshua 1:8).

But, don't get the idea that simply because this book focuses most of its attention on Biblical principles that it is a book of theory and not a book of practice. Because the Bible is itself by nature practical (Proverbs 3:5–6), this book is inevitably practical as well. In fact, we hope that it will prove to be helpful as a manual for action (James 1:22).

Christian philosopher Cornelius Van Til has said, "the Bible is authoritative on everything of which it speaks. And it speaks of everything." Even of such mundane matters as poverty and welfare. Thus, to evoke Scripture's blueprint for our cosmopolitan culture's complex dilemmas is not some naive resurrection of musty, dusty archaisms. "More than that, blessed are those who hear the word of God, and keep it!" (Luke 11:28) for, the Scripture cannot be broken" (John 10:35).

What does it profit, my brethren, if someone says he has faith but does not have deeds? Can that faith save him? If a brother or sister is naked and destitute of daily food, and one of you says to them, "Depart in peace, be warmed and filled," but you do not give them the things which are needed for the body, what does it profit? Thus also faith by itself, if it does not have deeds is dead.

James 2:14–17

1

WORD AND DEED EVANGELISM

> Also for Adam and his wife the LORD God made tunics of
> skin, and clothed them (Genesis 3:21).

Poverty is nothing new. It has plagued mankind from the very
beginning of time. Almost.

It all started in the garden.

Adam and Eve impoverished themselves amidst the riches of
Eden by sinning against God and transgressing His Law. Suddenly,
there in the shadow of plenty, they knew real poverty. They became
utterly destitute.

Pain and sorrow became their lot (Genesis 3:16). Hardship and
calamity became the course of their lives (Genesis 3:17) They fell
from riches to rags, from a well-watered garden to a progressively
more wretched wasteland (Genesis 3:18–19, 23–24).

When God came to them in the cool of the day, they were hud-
dled together in their misery and their shame (Genesis 3:7–8). He
looked upon their broken estate and saw their pitiful poverty.

So how did He respond to them? What did God do?

First, He pronounced a Word of judgement on them. He conducted a kind of courtroom lawsuit against them: questioning, inter-
rogating, cross-examining, and sentencing. He judged their sin
(Genesis 3:14–19).

Next, He pronounced a Word of hope for them. He opened the
prophetic books and revealed the promise of a Deliverer, a Savior.
He gave them good news (Genesis 3:15).

And finally, He confirmed His Word with deeds. He killed an
animal (or animals) and clothed them in the hides. He covered

8

them. He showed them mercy. He matched judgement and grace with charity (Genesis 3:21).

There in the cool of the garden, in the shadow of plenty, God confronted the sin of Adam and Eve. And He did it by meeting their deprivation with judgement first, good news second, and charity third.

This is the Biblical model, the divine model, of *true evangelism.*

True evangelism announces to sinful men that they have disobeyed a Holy God, that He will find them out, and that He will pronounce judgement against them.

True evangelism also offers hope. It tells sinful men that there is a Savior who crushes the serpent's head and redeems them from their plight.

But as essential as those two announcements are, true evangelism is not complete without charity. True evangelism involves both Word and deed.

God *verified* His Word of judgement and His Word of hope with sacrificial, merciful compassion. *That* is true evangelism.

When we proclaim the gospel to the nations, we must take great care to follow this model. If we fail to share God's abhorrence of sin and rebellion, we haven't truly evangelized. If we fail to share God's gracious provision of the cross of Christ, we haven't truly evangelized. This should be quite evident from the Scriptures. But at the same time, if we leave out the charity that *testifies* to the *ultimate charity* of God, then we haven't truly evangelized, either. That should be equally evident from the Scriptures.

Excuses, Excuses

Have you ever noticed the excuses that Adam and Eve gave for their sin?

Adam said, "The *woman* whom You gave to be with me, *she* gave me of the tree, and I ate" (Genesis 3:12). "Not me! It was her!"

Eve said, "The serpent deceived me and I ate" (Genesis 3:13). "Not me! It was him!"

Now in all fairness, neither of them actually lied. Both excuses were true. But they were *lame* excuses, nonetheless. Both sinners refused to face up to the fact: *They* had actually disobeyed God Almighty. They had no one to blame but themselves.

But blame they did: Adam blamed Eve, and Eve blamed the serpent.

Even that was not the worst of it, though. *Both of them also blamed God.* It was the woman *God* had given to him who was at fault, Adam said. In other words, "God, You messed up. You placed me in a poor environment. I was only responding to my circumstances. It's not my fault, God. It's *Your* fault!"

Eve said just about the same thing. "Look God, I was deceived. It wasn't my fault. I'm just a woman. This serpent here is very shrewd. Devilish, even. He knew just how to deceive the likes of me. So why did You let him into the garden? It's all *Your* fault. You should have known better than to let me be taken advantage off"

This sort of argument is the essence of sinful, rebellious poverty. Wherever it exists, there can be no escape from the downward spiral of want. If we refuse to regard ourselves as responsible agents before God, if we refuse to see our environment as something to be transformed by righteous labor, thrift, and planning for the future, then poverty of body and soul is our inescapable lot. If, like Adam and Eve, we insist that somebody else is responsible for our condition, then we will always be poor.

That is why God issues His Word of *judgement*. He will not let us excuse our sin. He forces us to accept personal responsibility for our sorry lot.

Grace and Charity

But God does not leave us under stern condemnation. He matches judgement with grace and charity.

Adam and Eve sinned. *Then* they tried to cover their sin by their own pitiful works: fig leaf aprons. *Then* they tried to hide from God. *Then* they tried to blame each other, or their environment, or God, or anyone but themselves.

They were deserving of death (Genesis 2:17; Romans 6:23). They had eaten the forbidden fruit. But God mercifully relented. Instead of immediately executing His holy wrath upon them, he graciously extended their lives.

And not only that, He graciously tended to their needs as well. He covered them.

God extended their lives by *grace*. He looked forward in time to the death of His Son Jesus, and He afforded them life for the sake of that ultimate sacrifice.

God covered their nakedness with *charity*. He looked forward in time to the robe of Christ's righteousness and He afforded them covering for the sake of that ultimate substitution.

God gave them *grace* (life). And God gave them *charity* (covering). Clearly, grace and charity are two sides of the same coin. Both come from the same root word in Greek: *charis.* Both flow forth from the mercy seat of Almighty God. Both are necessary to complete the work of evangelism begun by judgement.

God *gave*. Man received. Grace and charity quick on the heels of judgement. There was no legal obligation involved except the legal obligation that man trust and submit to God.

True evangelism always adheres to this pattern. It involves two clear messages: the coming judgement of God, and God's lawful way of escape in Christ the sin-bearer. Thus, the evangelist actually imitates God's pronouncement of judgement *against* the sinner and grace *to* the sinner when he preaches the gospel.

But if he stops there, he has not truly evangelized. Evangelism is not just words. It also involves deeds. It involves charity by the message-bearer, who imitates God's gift of the coverings to Adam and Eve. God is the model for judgement, grace, *and* charity.

Isaiah's Evangelism

We see this evangelical pattern in the testimony of the prophet Isaiah. He announces judgement. He announces a way of escape. And then he issues a call to charity.

Following God's model he said:

> Cry aloud, spare not; Lift up your voice like a trumpet; Declare to My people their transgression, And the house of Jacob their sins.... Is this not the fast that I have chosen: To loose the bonds of wickedness, To undo the heavy burdens, To let the oppressed go free, And that you break every yoke? Is it not to share your bread with the hungry, And that you bring to your house the poor who are cast out; When you see the naked, that you cover him, And not to hide yourself from your own flesh? Then your light will break out like the morning, Your healing shall spring forth speedily, And your righteousness shall go before you; The glory of the Lord shall be your rear guard. Then you shall call, and the Lord will answer; You shall cry, and He will say, "Here I am." If you take away the yoke from your midst, The pointing of the finger, and speaking wickedness, If you extend your soul to the hungry, And satisfy the afflicted soul Then your light shall dawn in the darkness, And your darkness shall be as the noonday. The Lord will guide you continually, And satisfy your soul in drought, And strengthen your bones; You shall be like a watered garden, And like a spring of water, whose waters do not fail. Those from among you shall build the old waste places; You shall raise up the foundations of many generations; And you shall be called the Repairer of the Breach, The Restorer of Streets to dwell in (Isaiah 58:1, 6–12).

God made His evangelistic program clear to Isaiah. *First,* he was to tell the people of Judah that they were in sin: "Declare to My people their transgression." *Second,* he was to reveal the way out: They were to fast in repentance. *Finally,* he was to point them toward righteous charity: They were not to starve themselves in a *ritual* fast, but to loosen the bonds of wickedness, to let the oppressed go free, to feed the hungry, to invite the homeless into their homes, to provide clothing for the naked.

Once again, here is God's plan of evangelism: First, announce the judgement of sin; second, proclaim the good news of hope; and third, take up the work of charity. First, *wrath against sin.* Second, *grace covering over* sin. And third, *charity soothing the hurts of sin.*

Christ's Evangelism

Jesus too confirmed this Word and deed pattern of evangelism. When He began His public ministry in the town of Nazareth, He went into the synagogue, as was His custom, and stood up to read. What He read was significant: the passage from Isaiah 61 that deals with the coming of the Messiah.

Who is the Messiah? The Anointed One who preaches the gospel to the poor:

> The Spirit of the Lord is upon Me, Because He has anointed Me to preach the gospel to the poor. He has sent Me to heal the brokenhearted, To preach deliverance to the captives, And recovery of sight to the blind, To set at liberty those who are oppressed, To preach the acceptable year of the Lord (Luke 4:18–19).

Isaiah had prophesied that the Anointed One would go into the highways and byways to heal the lame, to give sight to the blind, and to comfort the brokenhearted. Jesus proved His position as the Messiah by doing literally what Isaiah said He would do. So in the synagogue He boldly announced the prophetic fulfillment: "Today this Scripture is fulfilled in your hearing" (Luke 4:21).

Christ never shied away from announcing God's condemnation of sin (Matthew 7:13–23). Neither did He hesitate to announce the good news of hope (Matthew 11:28–30). But without acts of charity to back up those words, He would have seemed just another phony savior, just another false Christ.

Jesus proved He was the Messiah by wedding Word and deed. He authenticated His claims by combining judgement and grace with charity: He took liberty to the captives.

Charity was central to His ministry among us for this reason. He became poor for our sake, meting out charity because that was His Messianic task: to follow God's eternal pattern and save the perishing.

> For you know the grace of our Lord Jesus Christ, that though He was rich, yet for your sakes He became poor, that you through His poverty might become rich (2 Corinthians 8:9).

We owe everything to Christ. Our riches, however defined, come from Him. He experienced poverty to make our blessings possible. He became a servant for our sake. He exercised charity on our behalf.

And then came the ultimate charity: He suffered death and separation from God His Father for the sake of placating God's eternal wrath against us.

> He made Himself of no reputation, taking the form of a servant, and coming in the likeness of men. And being found in appearance as a man, He humbled Himself and became obedient to the point of death, even the death of the cross. Therefore God also has highly exalted Him and given Him the name which is above every name, that at the name of Jesus every knee should bow.... (Philippians 2:7–10).

Talk about serious charity! Yes, Jesus brought a message of judgement (Matthew 23:13–36). Yes, Jesus brought a message of great hope (Matthew 28:18–20). But He never let those words stand alone. He authenticated them with deeds.

What Does Charity Prove?

To challenge men with the gospel, we must first love them. Isaiah loved the people of Judah. He sacrificed his whole life to bring the message of salvation to those few who would listen. A man who has been loved by God is to show love to others: first, by proclaiming the coming judgement of God, second, by announcing His gracious escape, and third, by demonstrating commitment to God above, caring for the poor and helpless.

> Though I speak with the tongues of men and of angels, and have not charity, I am become as sounding brass, or a tinkling cymbal. And though I have the gift of prophecy, and understand all mysteries, and all knowledge; and though I have all faith, so that I could remove mountains, and have not charity, I am nothing. And though I bestow all my goods to feed the poor, and

though I give my body to be burned, and have not charity, it profiteth me nothing (1 Corinthians 13:1–3 KJV).

What did charity prove in the life of Jesus? It proved that He cared for men. It proved that He loved them. It proved that He was willing to put His life on the line. It proved that He was being fully obedient to His Father. Finally, it proved that His Words had *authority,* because they were being put into *action.*

Shortly after the announcement of His messianic authority in the synagogue at Nazareth, Jesus healed a paralyzed man. Jesus stood in front of the Pharisees and lawyers, who were watching to see if He would in any way commit a transgression of God's law. The paralyzed man had been brought to Him in a unique way: his friends had broken a hole in the roof and lowered him down, to avoid the crowd around Jesus.

> So when He saw their faith, He said to him, "Man, your sins are forgiven you." And the scribes and the Pharisees began to reason, saying, "Who is this who speaks blasphemies? Who can forgive sins but God alone?" But when Jesus perceived their thoughts, He answered and said to them, "Why are you reasoning in your hearts? Which is easier, to say, 'Your sins are forgiven you,' or to say, 'Rise up and walk'? But that you may know that the Son of Man has power on earth to forgive sins" He said to the man who was paralyzed, "I say to you, arise, take up your bed, and go to your house." Immediately he rose up before them, took up what he had been lying on, and departed to his own house, glorifying God. And they were all amazed, and they glorified God and were filled with fear, saying, We have seen strange things today! (Luke 5:20–26).

Jesus first drew attention to the man's sins. *Judgement.* Then He forgave him. *Grace.* And finally, in demonstration of His *authority* to judge and forgive, He raised the man *up. Charity.* Word was accompanied by deed.

Notice, that after Christ ministered to the man in this fashion the entire crowd was "amazed." They all "glorified God and were filled with fear." Seeing Word and deed *together,* they said with sheer astonishment, "We have seen strange things today."

Jesus *authenticated* the words of His mouth with the deeds of His hands. Jesus *demonstrated* the reality of His claims. And so the people *believed.*

Why does so much of our evangelism today have so little impact? Why do our best efforts so often fall on deaf ears? Could it be that we have strayed from God's pattern of evangelism? Could it be that we have stripped Gospel Word of its validity and authenticity by neglecting to accompany it with Gospel charity?

What does it profit, my brethren, if someone says he has faith but does not have deeds? Can that faith save him? If a brother or sister is naked and destitute of daily food, and one of you says to them, "Depart in peace, be warmed and filled," and you do not give them the things which are needed for the body, what does it profit? Thus also faith by itself, if it does not have deeds, is dead (James 2:14–17).

The world is looking for *proof.* They want *evidence.*

When Jesus wed Word and deed, the people who heard and saw got their proof. They needed no further evidence. They could see that this Gospel was not simply pie in the sky. It was a Gospel of hope. Real hope. It was a Gospel that made a *difference.*

Talk is cheap. True evangelism isn't.

Giving charity verifies the claims of the Gospel. It tells the world that there is indeed a sovereign gracious God who raises up faithful people, who blesses those people, and who gives them a loving disposition. It tells the world that there is a God who refills empty storehouses, replenishes dry cisterns, restocks depleted threshing floors, and opens hands and hearts. It tells the world that there is a God who instills such confidence in His followers that they can give, never fearing lack, that they can sacrifice, never lacking anything, that they can serve, never doubting provision. It provides proof.

Words of ultimate judgement and consummate hope need something to back them up in the eyes of sinful men. That "something" is charity.

Evangelism simply isn't complete if we fail to follow God's pattern of matching judgement and hope with charity.

Word and Deeds in History

Whenever and wherever the gospel has gone out, the faithful have emphasized the priority of good works, especially works of compassion toward the needy. They have matched the message of judgement and hope with charity. Every great revival in the history of the church, from Paul's missionary journeys to the Reformation, from Athanasius' Alexandrian outreach to America's Great Awakening, has been accompanied by an explosion of Christian care. Hospitals were established. Orphanages were founded. Rescue missions were started. Almshouses were built. Soup kitchens were begun. Charitable societies were incorporated. The hungry were fed, the naked clothed, and the homeless sheltered. Word was wed to deeds.

This fact has always proven to be the bane of the church's enemies. Apostates can argue theology. They can dispute philosophy. They can subvert history. And they can undermine character. But they are helpless in the face of the church's extraordinary feats of selfless compassion.

Not only did Augustine (354–430) change the face of the church with his brilliant theological treatises, he also transformed the face of Northern Africa, establishing works of charity in thirteen cities, modeling authentic Christianity for the whole of the Roman Empire.

Not only did Bernard of Clairveaux (1090–1153) launch the greatest monastic movement of all time, sparking evangelical fervor throughout France and beyond, he also established a charitable network throughout Europe to care for the poor, a network that has survived to this day.

Not only did John Wyclif (1320–1384) revive interest in the Scriptures during a particularly dismal and degenerate era with his translation of the New Testament into English, he also unleashed a grass-roots movement of lay preachers and relief workers that brought hope to the poor for the first time in over a century.

Not only did Jan Hus (1369–1415) shake the foundations of the medieval church hierarchy with his vibrant evangelistic sermons, he also mobilized a veritable army of workers for emergency relief at a time when central Europe was struck with one disaster after another.

Not only was John Calvin's (1509–1564) Geneva known throughout the world as the center of the Reformation, the hub of the greatest revival since Apostolic days, it was also renowned as a safe haven for all Europe's poor and persecuted, dispossessed, and distressed.

Not only was George Whitefield (1714–1770) the founder of Methodism (John Wesley was brought into the movement and then discipled by Whitefield) as well as the primary instigator of the Great Awakening in America, he was also the primary patron of Georgia's first orphanage and the driving force behind that colony's first relief association and hospital.

Not only was Charles Haddon Spurgeon (1834–1892) "the prince of the preachers" proclaiming the good news of "Christ and Him crucified" throughout Victorian England, he was also the founder of over 60 different charitable ministries including hospitals, orphanages, and almshouses.

Not only was Dwight L. Moody (1837–1899) America's premier evangelist throughout the dark days following the Civil War, he was also responsible for the establishment of over 150 street missions, soup kitchens, clinics, and rescue outreaches.

And on and on and on the story goes. From Francis of Assisi to Francis Schaeffer, from Polycarp to William Carey, obedient believers have always cared for the poor, the helpless, the orphan, and the widow. They wed word and deed.

For them, charity was, and is, central to the gospel task. And as a result, souls were saved, nations converted, and cultures restored. The message of their mouths was validated and authenticated by the work of their hands. The "peace that surpasses all understanding" became the inheritance of many because God's faithful covenant people kept His commandments.

Isaiah knew that. So did Augustine, Bernard, Wyclif, Hus, Calvin, Whitefield, Spurgeon, Moody, and countless others throughout the church's glorious march through the ages. They knew "that God is not one to show partiality, but in every nation the man who reveres Him and works righteousness, is welcome to Him" (Acts 10:34–35). And this is "the word which He sent to the sons of Israel, preaching peace through Jesus Christ" (Acts 10:36).

Thus, they knew that righteous deeds of compassion were essential for the fulfillment of the church's mission and could not be subjugated even to the most critical of tasks: discipleship, pastoral care, or cultural reclamation. They knew that the words of their mouths had to be authenticated by the works of their hands.

Faith at Work

In writing to Titus, the young pastor of Crete's pioneer church, the Apostle Paul pressed home this fundamental truth with impressive persistence and urgency. The task before Titus was not an easy one. Cretan culture was marked by deceit, ungodliness, sloth, and gluttony (Titus 1:12). And he was to provoke a total Christian reconstruction there! He was to introduce peace with God through Christ. Thus, Paul's instructions were strategically precise and to the point. Titus was to preach judgement and hope, but he was also to make good deeds the focus of his outreach. Charity was to be a central priority.

Paul wrote:

> For the grace of God that brings salvation has appeared to all men, teaching us that, denying ungodliness and worldly lusts,

we should live soberly, righteously, and godly in the present age, looking for the blessed hope and glorious appearing of our great God and Savior Jesus Christ, who gave Himself for us, that He might redeem us from every lawless deed and purify for Himself His own special people, zealous for good works (Titus 2:11–14).

Word *and* deed.

This was a very familiar theme for Paul. It wasn't exclusively aimed at the troublesome Cretan culture. Like Isaiah before him, he returned to it at every opportunity. Earlier, he had written to the Ephesian church saying,

For by grace you have been saved through faith, and that not of yourselves; it is the gift of God, not of works, lest anyone should boast. For we are His workmanship, created in Christ Jesus for good works, which God prepared beforehand that we should walk in them (Ephesians 2:8–10).

God saves us by grace. There is nothing we can do to merit His favor. We stand condemned under His judgement. Salvation is completely unearned (except by Christ), and undeserved (except to Christ). But we are not saved capriciously, for no reason and no purpose. On the contrary, "we are His workmanship, created in Christ Jesus for good works." We are "His own possession" set apart and purified to be "zealous for good deeds." Word and deed are inseparable. Judgement is answered with grace. Grace is answered with charity. This is the very essence of the evangelistic message.

So, Paul tells Titus he must order his fledgling ministry among the Cretans accordingly. He himself was "to be a pattern of good deeds" (Titus 2:7). He was to teach the people "to be ready for every good work" (Titus 3:1). The older women and the younger women were to be thus instructed, so "that the word of God may not be dishonored" (Titus 2:5); and the bondslaves, "that they may adorn the doctrine of God our Savior in all things" (Titus 2:10). They were all to "learn to maintain good works, to meet urgent needs, that they may not be unfruitful" (Titus 3:14). There were those within the church who professed "to know God, but in works they deny Him, being abominable, disobedient, and disqualified for every good work" (Titus 1:16). These, Titus was to "rebuke … sharply, that they may be sound in the faith" (Titus 1:13). He was to "affirm constantly, that those who have believed in God should be careful to maintain good works" (Titus 3:8).

As a pastor, Titus had innumerable tasks that he was responsible to fulfill. He had administrative duties (Titus 1:5), doctrinal duties (Titus 2:1), discipling duties (Titus 2:2–10), preaching duties

(Titus 2:15), counseling duties (Titus 3:1–2), and arbitrating duties (Titus 3:12–13). But intertwined with them all, fundamental to them all, were his *charitable* duties.

And what was true for Titus then is true for us all today, for "these things are good and profitable for all men" (Titus 3:8 KJV).

Isaiah knew that. So did Augustine, Bernard, Wyclif, and the others. True evangelism weds *word and deed*. It always has. It always will.

The Bible tells us that if we would obey the command to be generous to the poor, we would ourselves be happy (Proverbs 14:21), God would preserve us (Psalm 41:1–2), we would never suffer need (Proverbs 28:27), we would prosper and be satisfied (Proverbs 11:25), and even be raised up from beds of affliction (Psalm 41:3). God would ordain peace for us (Isaiah 26:12), bless us with peace (Psalm 29:11), give us His peace (John 14:27), guide our feet into the way of peace (Luke 1:79), ever and always speaking peace to us (Psalm 85:8), and grant peace to the land (Leviticus 26:6). God would authenticate our faith, our evangelistic message (James 2:14–26).

Therefore let us be "zealous for good works" (Titus 2:14).

From Pillar to Post

Sadly, like the Israelites in Isaiah's day, and the Cretans to whom Titus was commissioned to minister, we have turned away from true evangelism to pursue our own twisted agendas.

As it is written, "There is none righteous, no not one; There is none who understands; There is none who seeks for God. They have all gone out of the way; They have together become unprofitable; There is none who does good, no, not one. Their throat is an open tomb; With their tongues they have practiced deceit; The poison of asps is under their lips; Whose mouth is full of cursing and bitterness. Their feet are swift to shed blood; Destruction and misery are in their ways; And the way of peace have they not known. There is no fear of God before their eyes" (Romans 3:10–18).

Our tendency has been to alternate between sanctimonious escapism and humanistic activism. And *neither* represents the Scriptural position. We have either adopted a know-nothing-do-nothing *pietism* that makes us so heavenly minded that we're no earthly good, or a save-the-starving-third-world-whales bleeding-heart *liberalism* that separates us from the problems God has put on our own doorsteps.

Charity is central to the task of evangelism, but we have run from pillar to post, from extreme to extreme with all manner of needless, heedless extravagance. We have perpetrated self-promoting trivialities, self-indulgent mundanities, and self-serving inanities while the nations of the earth languish and perish, never knowing the glorious hope of Christ our Lord.

If we are to have any hope of faithfully fulfilling the Great Commission, if we are ever to "lay hold of the good things of the Lord" (1 Timothy 6:19), then we must begin, "... to loosen the bonds of wickedness, to undo the bands of the yoke, and to let the oppressed go free ... to divide ... bread with the hungry, and bring the homeless poor into the house ..." (Isaiah 58:6–7 NAS).

We cannot afford to play games any longer. There is starving in the shadow of plenty. Young and old, black and white, male and female, the dispossessed cry out. Their voices arise from wretched backwoods hovels in Appalachia, from crime-ridden streets in Philadelphia, from frozen alleyways in Baltimore, from rat-infested tenements in Harlem, from gutted public housing projects in Dallas.

We must answer those voices. With God's Word of judgement. With God's Word of hope. And with God's hand of charity.

Conclusion

The first basic principle in the Biblical blueprint for welfare is that charity completes the work of evangelism. It is *integral* to the evangelistic mandate.

We will never know the full blessings of peace, abundance, and joy that God intends for His faithful people unless we understand this. In fact, we can't even claim to be His faithful people unless we understand this. Righteous good deeds are the unavoidable results of a life yielded to Christ. They are the fruits of grace. They authenticate, verify, and give evidence to the work of the Spirit. They go hand in hand with the proclaimed Word.

A quick glance at church history shows that this has been the understanding of Christ's disciples throughout all times, eras, and dispensations. So though discipleship, missions, pastoral care, and education have always occupied the church's attentions, charity has maintained its priority place of adorning the doctrine of truth with grace and love. Without charity, discipleship, pastoral care, and education are hollow and incomplete; they are unable to get started.

Charity is integral to the fulfillment of the Great Commission. Evangelism is weakened without it. In fact, evangelism is not true evangelism without it.

Summary

God responded to the sin of Adam and Eve first by announcing *judgement*, second, by proclaiming *hope*, and third, by extending *charity*.

This divine pattern of wedding word and deed is the Biblical model of true evangelism.

In his evangelistic message to the Israelites, Isaiah followed this pattern, condemning sin, calling for repentance, and outlining a life-style of righteous good deeds.

Jesus too, followed this same pattern, fulfilling the Messianic prophesies that foretold His integration of *Word and deed*.

Thus, when the early Christians began to take the Gospel to the nations, they naturally adhered to the pattern as well. From Titus in Crete to Spurgeon in London, the story has always been the same: charity authenticates the evangelistic message; without it revival tarries.

If we are to ignite the fires of holy devotion and evangelistic effectiveness, then we too must return to this very fundamental truth: *faith without deeds is dead*. Our faithful fulfillment of the Great Commission depends on it.

2

THE SAMARITAN LEGACY

And behold, a certain lawyer stood up and tested Him, saying, "Teacher, what shall I do to inherit eternal life?" He said to
him, "What is written in the law? What is your reading of it?" So
he answered and said, "You shall love the Lord your God with all
your heart, with all your soul, with all your strength, and with all
your mind," and "your neighbor as yourself." And He said to
him, "You have answered rightly; do this, and you *will* live" (Luke
10:25–28).

It was supposed to be a test. Straightforward. Simple. A test of
orthodoxy. A test of theological skillfulness. Not a trap, really, just a
test.

"You shall love the Lord your God ..." Jesus said,   and   your
neighbor..."

Well, so far, so good. Christ's Sunday School-word-perfect-
never-miss-a-beat response should have been music to the ears of
any good Pharisee. He unhesitatingly upheld the Mosaic Law. He
was careful "not to exceed what is written" (1 Corinthians 4:6). He
was impeccably orthodox.

If that were the end of the story, it would be less a story than a
dry recitation of doctrine: true, good, and necessary, but not particularly gripping. But of course, the story *doesn't* end there. It goes on:
true, good, necessary, *and* gripping.

The lawyer just wouldn't let Jesus off the hook. He continued to
cross-examine the Lord. He pressed the issue. Sinful men love to do
this. They want God on the hot seat. They want God in the dock.

Jesus wouldn't make *him* look like a fool!

But he wanting to justify himself, said to Jesus, "And who is my neighbor?" Then Jesus answered and said: "A certain man went down from Jerusalem to Jericho, and fell among thieves, who stripped him of his clothing, wounded him, and departed, leaving him half dead. Now by chance a certain priest came down that road. And when he saw him, he passed by on the other side. Likewise a Levite, when he arrived at the place, came and looked, and passed by on the other side. But a certain Samaritan, as he journeyed, came where he was. And when he saw him, he had compassion on him, and went to him and bandaged his wounds, pouring on oil and wine; and he set him on his own animal, brought him to an inn, and took care of him. On the next day, when he departed, he took out two denarii, gave them to the innkeeper, and said to him, 'Take care of him; and whatever more you spend, when I come again, I will repay you,' So which of these three do you think was neighbor to him who fell among the thieves?" And he said, "He who showed mercy on him." Then Jesus said to him, "Go and do likewise" (Luke 10:29-37).

Quite a story! What started out to be a test, a theological confrontation over the law, was suddenly transformed by the Lord Jesus into a moment of conviction. The Pharisee found himself in the valley of decision. And at the same time he was on the horns of a dilemma.

A Samaritan! How odd!

Seven hundred years earlier, Assyria had overrun and depopulated the northern kingdom of Israel, including Samaria. The conquerors had a cruel policy of population transfer that scattered the inhabitants of the land to the four winds. Then, the empty countryside was repopulated with a ragtag collection of vagabonds and scalawags from the dregs of the Empire (2 Kings 17:24-41). Instead of regarding these newcomers as prospects for Jewish evangelism, the people of Judah, who continued in independence for another full century, turned away in contempt, and the racial division between Samaritan and Jew began its bitter course.

Samaritans were universally despised by good Jews. They were half-breeds who observed a half-breed religious cultus. Worse than the pagan Greeks, worse even than the barbarian Romans, the Samaritans were singled out by Jews as a perfect example of despicable depravity. They were close enough geographically and culturally to know the Pharisees' version of the truth, yet they resisted. They had no excuse; other nations did. They were therefore far more guilty than other nations. At least in the eyes of the Jews.

And now, Jesus was elevating a Samaritan, of all things, to a position of great respect and honor. A Samaritan was the good neighbor, the hero of the parable.

Jesus was slapping the religious leaders of Israel in their collective faces.

After demanding an expansion of Christ's textbook answer, the teacher might have expected a parable that encouraged him to show love to all men, *even* to Samarians. But never in a thousand years would he have guessed that Christ would show how such a despised one could be nearer to the Kingdom than a pious, but compassionless Jew.

The teacher asked a *passive* question, expecting a *passive* answer: "Who is my neighbor?" (Luke 10:29). But Jesus responded with an *active* command: "Go and do likewise." (Luke 10:37). In other words, Jesus did not supply the teacher with *information* about whom he should or shouldn't help, because failure to keep the commandment springs not from a lack of information, but a lack of *obedience* and *love*. It was not keener understanding that the teacher needed, but a new heart. Like that of the Samaritan!

Both Law and Love

The Samaritan in the story is a paragon of virtue. He strictly observed the Law, shaming the priest and Levite who "passed by on the other side" (Luke 10:31–32). He paid attention to the needs of others (Deuteronomy 22:4) and showed concern for the poor (Psalm 41:1). He showed pity toward the weak (Psalm 72:13) and rescued them from violence (Psalm 72:14). Knowing the case of the helpless (Proverbs 29:7), he gave of his wealth (Deuteronomy 26:12–13), and shared his food (Proverbs 22:9).

But perhaps even more significant than his strict adherence to the Law was the *compassion* that the Samaritan demonstrated. He wasn't simply "going by the rules." His was not a dry, passionless obedience. He had "put on tender mercies, kindness, humbleness of mind, meekness, longsuffering" (Colossians 3:12). He "became a father to the poor, and searched out the case" of the stranger (job 29:16). He loved his neighbor as himself (Mark 12:31), thus fulfilling the Law (Romans 13:10).

The Samaritan fulfilled the demands of both Law and love! He demonstrated both obedience and compassion, holding to *both* the Spirit and the letter. He had wed Word and deed.

There were established structures, built into the cultural framework of Israel, for the care of the needy. There were provisions for free harvesting (Leviticus 19:9–10; Deuteronomy 24:19–22). There were alms feasts (Deuteronomy 14:22–29) and alms giving (Deuteronomy 26:12–13). There were debt cancellations (Deuteronomy 15:1–11) and special loans available (Leviticus 25:35–55).

But there wasn't any time to call a community meeting. There wasn't time to go through all the official channels, or make a formal request. There was simply a man lying in the road who was so near death that the religious representatives of Israel were afraid of touching him, for fear of coming under the Old Testament Laws regarding contact with a dead body (Numbers 19:11–16). Why, it might have required them to go through some inconvenient ritual washing requirements! No, better to let the man lie there.

The Samaritan refuses to "pass the buck." He isn't worried about contact with the dead, for he honors a basic principle of life: charity. He refuses to leave the "dirty work"—the ritually unclean work—to someone else. He accepts personal responsibility, never once looking for an easy way out. He spends *his* time, *his* money, and *his* energy on behalf of the poor man.

Thinking perhaps that someone else would come along—someone better equipped, someone "called" to that kind of outreach— just someone else; the priest and the Levite "did not remember to show mercy" (Psalm 109:16), but the Samaritan rescued "the poor and needy" to "free them from the hand of the wicked" (Psalm 82:4). Without hesitation. Without a second thought. Without looking for excuses. He just did his job. He did what he *ought* to have done. He did what he *had* to do morally. He demonstrated Law *and* love in action.

He realized that charity was part of the job of righteousness, of evangelism. And it was his job. There was no way around it.

It didn't matter what the priest did or didn't do. It didn't matter what the Levite did or didn't do. It only mattered that God had encoded compassion into His unchangeable Word and that He had caused the Samaritan to cross paths with the victim pilgrim.

Charity was *his* job.

A Model for the Church

When the early Christians read or heard the story of the Good Samaritan, they were devastated, as Jesus knew they would be. This went beyond Law-keeping! Real spiritual power would be needed to imitate the Good Samaritan, and they knew that "with men it was impossible"—until that is, they realized just Who the Good Samaritan really was.

You see, by itself this story only condemns us. Who is equal to the task? Only *the* Good Samaritan, Jesus Himself (see John 8:48), a man from "Galilee of the *gentiles*," (Matthew 4:15). Like the God-fearing Samaritans of 2 Chronicles 28:8–15, Jesus had come to "free the captives."

The early Christians realized that what the Law could not do (the priest and the Levite), Jesus had done. After all, the priest had a legitimate worry: Contact with an unclean person would defile him and prevent him from exercising his appointed task. But Jesus had broken the restrictions of the ceremonial Law. A new age had come!

The early Christians also realized that the inn in the parable was the church, and the innkeeper symbolized pastors. But more than that, they realized that the Holy Spirit had been poured out, placing them in ethical *union* with Christ the Good Samaritan, and *enabling* them to imitate His grace and mercy.

The parable no longer condemned them. Rather, it liberated them to do deeds of love and mercy, by which the heavenly Kingdom would come.

The faith of the Good Samaritan became a model for the church ever after. Taking their cue from him, the faithful saints of the Gospel's pioneer days took responsibility for the needy in their midst with an eagerness and effectiveness that utterly baffled the populace at large. Having sole access to the "bread of life" (John 6:48), they knew that if *they* did not feed the masses of starving souls in their day, *no one* would. They were driven by a holy compulsion.

Luke tells us of the liberality of the Jerusalem church, led by the remarkably charitable Barnabas.

> And with great power the apostles gave witness to the resurrection of the Lord Jesus. And great grace was upon them all. Nor was there anyone among them who lacked; for all who were possessors of lands or houses sold them, and brought the proceeds of the things that were sold, and laid them at the apostles' feet; and they distributed to each as anyone had need. And Joses, who was also named Barnabas by the apostles (which is translated Son of Encouragement), a Levite of the country of Cyprus, having land, sold it, and brought the money and laid it at the apostles' feet (Acts 4:33–37).

Writing to the Corinthians, Paul describes the Good Samaritan attributes of the Macedonian Church.

> Moreover, brethren, we make known to you the grace of God bestowed on the churches of Macedonia: that in a great trial of affliction the abundance of their joy and their deep poverty

abounded in the riches of their liberality. For I bear witness that according to their ability, yes, and beyond their ability, they were freely willing, imploring us with much urgency that we would receive the gift and the fellowship of the ministering to the saints. And this they did, not as we had hoped, but first gave themselves to the Lord, and then to us by the will of God (2 Corinthians 8:1–5).

And the Good Samaritan faith was imitated by scores of others, both churches and individuals, throughout the New Testament era: Tabitha (Acts 9:36–41), Titus (2 Corinthians 8:16–17), Paul (Acts 11:27–30), Peter and James (Galatians 2:9–10), Phoebe (Romans 16:1–2), Stephanas, Fortunatus, and Achaicus (1 Corinthians 16:17–18), Philemon (Philemon 5), Epaphroditus (Philippians 2:25–30), the church in Thyatira (Revelation 2:19), Tychicus (Ephesians 6:21–22), and Cornelius (Acts 10:31). One and all, they demonstrated the reality of their faith with selfless compassion. Like the Good Samaritan, they fulfilled the demands of both Law and love. Like Him, they realized that charity was part of the job of righteousness, of evangelism. And it was their job.

It was *their* job. Not the civil government's. Not the bureaucracy's. Not the Pharisees'. Not the Sanhedrin's. Not the Romans' or the Greeks' or the Jews'. It was *their* job.

It was a job no one else could do.

And because they did it, they were able to conquer the Roman Empire in less than three centuries.

God's Own Provision

God's people have always been cared for by God's own hand.

When they have been homeless, He has given them shelter. For instance, when Abraham was nothing but a wandering shepherd, the Lord made a covenant with him saying,

> ...To your descendants I have given this land, from the river of Egypt to the great river, the River Euphrates—the Kenites, the Kenizzites, and the Kadmonites; the Hittites, the Perizzites, and the Rephaim; the Amorites, the Canaanites, the Girgashites, and the Jebusites (Genesis 15:18–21).

When his descendants were driven from their homes by famine, God moved the heart of Pharaoh in Egypt to open his land to the Jews saying,

> Now you are commanded—do this: take carts out of the land of Egypt for your little ones and for your wives; bring your father

and come. Also do not be concerned about your goods, for the best of all the land of Egypt is yours (Genesis 45:19–20).

Later, when conditions in Egypt made life unbearable for the people, God promised them a new home, a land flowing with milk and honey.

And the Lord said: "I have surely seen the oppression of My people who are in Egypt, and have heard their cry because of their taskmasters, for I know their sorrows. So I have come down to deliver them out of the hand of the Egyptians, and to bring them up from that land to a good and large land, to a land flowing with milk and honey, to the place of the Canaanites and the Hittites and the Amorites and the Perizzites and the Hivites and the Jebusites. Now therefore, behold, the cry of the children of Israel has come to Me, and I have also seen the oppression with which the Egyptians oppress them. Come now, therefore, and I will send you to Pharaoh that you may bring My people, the children of Israel, out of Egypt" (Exodus 3:7–10).

Whenever the people were exiled, alone, in a dry and weary wasteland, God came to their rescue and gave them shelter.

A father of the fatherless, a defender of widows, is God in His holy habitation. God sets the solitary in families; He brings out those who are bound into prosperity; But the rebellious dwell in a dry land. (Psalm 68:5–6)

So, throughout the ages, His people have cried out in praise, saying,

I will love You, O Lord, my strength. The Lord is my rock and my fortress and my deliverer; My God, my strength, in whom I will trust; My shield and the horn of my salvation, my stronghold. I will call upon the Lord, who is worthy to be praised; So shall I be saved from my enemies (Psalm 18:1–3).

But, not only have they raised up songs of joyous praise, they have been provoked to shelter the homeless themselves. Having tasted the abundance of God's lovingkindness, they felt compelled to minister likewise to others. They became "Good Samaritans." They asserted along with the Apostle Paul the necessity of giving that which they had been given.

Blessed be the God and Father of our Lord Jesus Christ, the Father of mercies and God of all comfort, who comforts us in all our tribulation, that we may be able to comfort those who are in any trouble, with the comfort with which we ourselves are comforted by God. For as the sufferings of Christ abound in us, so also our consolation also abounds through Christ (2 Corinthians 1:3–5).

They cared for the alien, the stranger, the sojourner, the weak, the poor, and the despised because they once had been in that deprived state themselves and God had graciously raised them up (Exodus 22:21–24, 23:9; Leviticus 19:32–34).

God's "Good Samaritan" people shelter the dispossessed because they themselves have been sheltered.

Similarly, when they have been hungry, God has fed them. He fed them in the garden (Genesis 2:16). He fed them manna in the desert (Exodus 16:4). He fed them bread in the morning and meat in the evening (Exodus 16:12). He fed them on the fat of a bounteous land flowing with grapes, figs, and pomegranates, flowing with milk and honey (Numbers 13:23–27). He fed them in times of famine (Ruth 1:1–6), in times of oppression (Ezekiel 34:13–14), in times of distress (1 Kings 19:1–8), in times of drought (1 Kings 17:1–16), and in times of war (1 Samuel 21:1–6).

The Lord will not allow the righteous soul to famish" (Proverbs 10:3).

When Jesus, the real Good Samaritan came, He came *to feed.* The people were starving. So Jesus fed them. He fed them loaves and fishes (John 6:1–14). And He fed them the "bread of life" (John 6:33). He said to them, "I am the bread of life. He who comes to Me shall never hunger, and he who believes in Me shall never thirst" (John 6:35). He continued, saying,

> Most assuredly, I say to you, he who believes in Me has everlasting life. I am the Bread of life. Your fathers ate the manna in the wilderness, and are dead. This is the bread which comes down from heaven, that one may eat of it and not die. I am the living bread which came down from heaven. If anyone eats of this bread, he will live forever; and the bread that I shall give is My flesh, which I shall give for the life of the world (John 6:47–51).

Clearly, "this is a hard saying; who can understand it?" (John 6:60). But one thing is very evident. Jesus came to feed the starving. He came to invite us to His banqueting table (1 Corinthians 11:23–25). He came to sup with us, and us with Him (Revelation 3:20). He came to prepare a table before us in the presence of our enemies, to anoint our heads with oil, and to fill our cups to overflowing (Psalm 23:5). He came to feed us at the glorious marriage supper of the Lamb (Revelation 19:7–9).

Ever since, Christians have made the focus of their weekly worship the Lord's Supper. They have come together to eat. God gathers His people about Him and feeds them from His bounty.

As a result, God's "Good Samaritans" in turn feed the hungry because they themselves have been fed. And because of that, they are the *only* ones capable of feeding. They are the *only* ones who have partaken of God's own provision. They are the *only* ones to have been truly sheltered, truly fed. They are the *only* ones to have learned genuine refuge, genuine nourishment. And they are the *only* ones to have before their eyes constant reminders of that provision: the land of promise, and the memorial communion.

God's people are the only ones fit for "Good Samaritan" service because they are the only ones fit by "Good Samaritan" service.

Christians are supposed to exercise dominion over the whole earth (Genesis 1:28; Matthew 28:19–20). It is their job—an assignment from God that they and they alone will be equipped to fulfill in eternity. But power *and* authority come through service. There is no more fundamental principle of dominion in the Bible. Charity is the first step toward reformation and victory (Isaiah 58:10–12).

From the Table of the Lord

Historically, Christians have cared for the poor, remembering their own care from above. And they have particularly remembered this in connection with the Lord's Supper. The Free Presbyterian Church of Scotland has for 'centuries now provided for almsgiving immediately following the communion meal. Likewise, the Christian Reformed churches traditionally have a special offering for the poor after the quarterly Lord's Supper service. Primitive Baptists make special provision for charitable offerings as the communion elements are passed, that all may feast. The historic liturgical churches take up food and clothing during the Christmas and Easter Eucharists, so that the abundance of God's table might be shared, with even those along the highways and hedges (Luke 14:16–24). For, "Blessed is he who shall eat bread in the Kingdom of God" (Luke 14:15).

This special integration of physical and spiritual concerns is possible only among God's people. Bureaucracies can't even begin to provide the holistic care to the poor that the church can. Neither can governments or other secular coalitions and associations.

Thus, it is terribly tragic when the church loses sight of all this. When the church minimizes the Lord's Supper to make room for "more important" matters, when she attempts to separate "worldly" affairs from "heavenly" affairs, when she makes a distinction between "the sacred" and "the profane," when she underplays "social" issues in favor of "spiritual" issues, when she delegates its responsibility to care for the poor to others, she becomes like salt that has lost its savor (Matthew 5:13). She abandons the Great Commission to win all things for the Lord Jesus (Matthew 28:18–20). She no longer attempts to "bring all things in heaven and on earth together under one Head, even Christ" (Ephesians 1:10). She plays into the hands of the enemies of the truth (1 Peter 5:8). She fails to recognize that charity is an essential component in the work of the Gospel.

With such scrambled priorities, is it any wonder that our evangelism has bogged down? Is it any wonder that worldliness has crept into our churches almost unnoticed? Is it any wonder that our youth wander away from the fold into the house of horrors that American culture has become? Is it any wonder that our families are disintegrating, that our schools are in shambles, and that humanism has captured control of the media, the courts, and the arts? Is it? Is it any wonder that our streets and alleys and parks are cluttered with the human refuse of an economy gone mad? Is it?

Not hardly.

When the people of God forget who they are; when they forget what they are supposed to do; when they forget who they serve and for what purpose, then all the world suffers. "Where there is no vision, the people perish" (Proverbs 29:18 KJV).

The very foundations of our life and liberty are at risk because we *have* forgotten. And, "If the foundations are destroyed, what can the righteous do?" (Psalm 11:3).

What can we do?

Well, it's simple. We do our job.

We "build the old waste places," and we "raise up the foundations of many generations," and we "repair the breach," and we "restore the streets in which to dwell" (Isaiah 58:12).

And how do we do that?

Again, it's simple. We do our job.

We "give ourselves to the hungry," and we "satisfy the desire of the afflicted" (Isaiah 58:10).

That's all.

But of course, that's plenty. And that's what leads to plenty.

Conclusion

The second basic principle in the Biblical blueprint for welfare is that charity *is our* job. It is the job of Christians.

The Good Samaritan modeled for the church compassion and charity. He came as a reminder that because God has cared for us, we are to care for the afflicted of the world. He came as a sign of all that Christ has done for us, and the responsibility that has resulted. Jesus came to feed His people on the bread of life, and now we are in turn to feed the needy from that bounty. We are to integrate spiritual and physical concerns, meeting the needs of the *whole* man. This is one of the special dynamics of the Lord's Supper celebration.

The Good Samaritan didn't wait. He didn't shuffle his responsibility off on someone else. He understood that *he* would have to care for the victim by the way with the very care he had received from Almighty God.

Can we do any less?

Summary

The story of the Good Samaritan, as shocking as it was to Christ's interrogator, was a classic defense of the Old Testament faith, the faith of Abraham, Isaac, Jacob, Moses, David, and all the prophets: Law and love.

The Hero in the story—who was in fact Christ Himself—refused to evade His very clear responsibility to authenticate His Words with deeds.

The early Christians by the power of the Holy Spirit used the Good Samaritan as a model for their own works of righteousness: making certain that there were no needy among them, caring for the orphans and widows, and sacrificially giving to various relief causes.

They knew that charity was *their job* and no one else's because only they were qualified, only they had been cared for by God Himself.

The Lord's Supper emblemizes the fact that God cares for our most basic and fundamental needs and that we are to likewise go to the world caring for the needs of others. That's our job.

The challenge that faces us then is quite simple: Do our job; Adhere to the Samaritan Legacy.

3

DOMINION BY SERVICE

Ahaz was twenty years old when he became king, and he reigned sixteen years in Jerusalem; and he did not do what was right in the sight of the Lord, as his father David had done.... Therefore the Lord his God delivered him into the hand of the king of Syria. They defeated him, and carried away a great multitude of them as captives, and brought them to Damascus. Then he was also delivered into the hand of the king of Israel, who defeated him with a great slaughter. For Pekah the son of Remaliah killed one hundred and twenty thousand in Judah in one day, all valiant men, because they had forsaken the Lord God of their fathers. Zichri, a mighty man of Ephraim, killed Maaseiah the king's son, Azrikam the officer over the house, and Elkanah who was second to the king. And the children of Israel carried away captive of their brethren two hundred thousand women, sons, and daughters; and they also took away much spoil from them, and brought the spoil to Samaria (2 Chronicles 28:1, 5–8).

He was just trying to save his skin. And there didn't seem to be any other way. With enemy armies to the left of him and enemy armies to the right of him, any help seemed like good help. He was grasping at straws.

Apparently, early on in Ahaz's reign, Rezin, king of Aram (Syria), and Pekah, king of Israel, tried to force him to join their defensive alliance against Assyria (Isaiah 7:1). Failing to persuade him, they decided to invade Jerusalem (2 Kings 16:5). The young king's army suffered heavy casualties and many of his subjects were dragged off into captivity.

What should the young king do? Where should he turn? Whom could he trust?

Then the Lord said to Isaiah, "Go out now to meet Ahaz, you and Shear-Jashub your son, at the end of the aqueduct from the upper pool, on the highway to the Fuller's field, and say to him: 'Take heed, and be quiet; do not fear or be fainthearted for these two stubs of smoking firebrands, for the fierce anger of Rezin and Syria, and the son of Remaliah. Because Syria, Ephraim, and the son of Remaliah have taken evil counsel against you, saying, "Let us go up against Judah and trouble it, and let us make a gap in its wall for ourselves, and set a king over them, the son of Tabeel"—'Thus says the Lord God, "It shall not stand, Nor shall it come to pass. For the head of Syria is Damascus, and the head of Damascus is Rezin. Within sixty-five years Ephraim will be broken, So that it will not be a people. The head of Ephraim is Samaria, And the head of Samaria is Remaliah's son. If you will not believe, surely you shall not be established"' (Isaiah 7:3–9).

In the midst of the crisis, Isaiah came to the king beseeching him to put his trust in the Lord. Though his armies be defeated, though his city be besieged, though his hopes be dashed, Ahaz could rely on the faithfulness of the King of kings. He could turn unto Him. After all, what was Rezin before the awesome glory of the Almighty God? What was Pekah before the sovereign Maker of heaven and earth? Ahaz could rest and relax. He could wait in silent confidence for God to rescue him from his adversaries (Psalm 7:1), for the Lord would be his rock and his salvation, his stronghold in times of calamity (Psalm 62:2). The Lord Himself would be a shield about him, the glory and the lifter of his head (Psalm 3:3).

But no, that wasn't sufficient for faithless Ahaz. He wanted something "more secure" than the promise of divine intervention, divine favor. So …

At the same time King Ahaz sent to the kings of Assyria to help him (2 Chronicles 28:16).

God's way wasn't good enough for Ahaz. In fact, God himself wasn't good enough for Ahaz. He preferred the throne of Nineveh to the throne of heaven. He preferred the strength of mere men to the strength of the hosts of glory.

And for that grave error in judgement, he paid dearly. For the rest of his life, he paid.

"Woe to the rebellious children," says the Lord, "Who take counsel, but not of Me, And devise plans, but not of My Spirit, That they may add sin to sin" (Isaiah 30:1).

Because he entered into an unholy alliance, because he chose to trust in men and their schemes rather than God and His covenant promises, Ahaz wreaked havoc upon his tiny kingdom.

Rezin and Pekah were driven back finally, but for that service the pagan kings of Assyria charged a monumental tribute that virtually emptied the royal treasury (2 Chronicles 28:21). Ahaz even had to resort to pilfering the Temple in order to pay off his debt to the warlords of Nineveh for their newly enforced "peace" (2 Chronicles 28:20–21). Ahaz placed an Assyrian altar in the temple court (2 Kings 16:10–14) and displaced the original bronze altar, utilizing it for divination (2 Kings 16:15). Eventually, he even closed the Temple sanctuary itself, preferring the "high places" of the newly installed pagan cult (2 Chronicles 28:24–25), completely desecrating all worship of the Lord (2 Kings 16:17–18).

And that wasn't even the half of it. As it turned out, Assyria wasn't a very good ally, even after all the expense, heartache, and spiritual compromise. When the Edomites and the Philistines decided to take advantage of Judah's weakened condition, the high and mighty in Nineveh simply ignored the situation and allowed Ahaz to be sacked mercilessly (2 Chronicles 28:17–19).

Service and Authority

There is a fundamental principle of dominion in the Bible: *dominion through service*. This principle is understood well by the modern welfare State. The politicians and planners recognize that the agency that supplies charity in the name of the people will gain the allegiance of the people. So, they "serve." And so they gain dominion.

The kings of the Gentiles exercise lordship over them, and those who exercise authority over them are called "benefactors." But not so among you; on the contrary, he who is greatest among you, let him be as the younger, and he who governs as he who serves. For who is greater, he who sits at the table, or he who serves? Is it not he who sits at the table? Yet I am among you as the One who serves. But you are those who have continued with Me in My trials. And I bestow upon you a kingdom, just as My Father bestowed one upon Me, that you may eat and drink at My table in My kingdom, and sit on thrones judging the twelve tribes of Israel (Luke 22:25–30).

Unfortunately, Christians have not understood this link between charity and authority. They have time and again fallen into the trap that snared Ahaz: alliances with the enemy.

Someone must be in charge. There is no escape from responsibility. When people are needy, or fearful, or desperate, they seek protection. Who will give it to them? And what will the protector, the benefactor, ask in return?

This is why the question of the responsibility for charity is ultimately a question of authority. And this is why the issue of charity is such a volatile issue. At stake is ultimate control over the society. For that men will go to war.

Thus, the battle for the control over charity is very similar to a military campaign. And God's people are warned repeatedly by God: make no alliance with foreign gods. Make no alliances with the enemy.

Unholy Alliances

God's warnings against entering into unholy alliances are abundant and clear.

> Do not enter the path of the wicked, And do not walk in the way of evil. Avoid it, do not travel on it; Turn away from it and pass on. For they do not sleep unless they have done evil; And their sleep is taken away unless they make someone fall. For they eat the bread of wickedness, And drink the wine of violence. But the path of the just is like the shining sun, that shines ever brighter unto the perfect day. The way of the wicked is like darkness; They do not know what makes them stumble (Proverbs 4:14–19).

When the Israelites came out of the land of Egypt, He emphasized the issue.

> Observe what I command you this day. Behold, I am driving out from before you the Amorite and the Canaanite and the Hittite and the Perizzite and the Hivite and the Jebusite. Take heed to yourself, lest you make a covenant with the inhabitants of the land where you are going, lest it be a snare in your midst (Exodus 34:11–12).

The problem was not so much that the pagan influences of the other nations would pollute God's covenant people, though it is true that "Bad company corrupts good morals" (1 Corinthians 15:33). The real problem was that God *desired that the people rely on Him, and Him alone.* For their security, for their guidance, for their inspiration, for their standards of good and evil, of right and wrong, of beauty and knowledge, of pleasure and wisdom. God was to be entirely sufficient, their only source of help and hope.

Blessed is the man Who does not walk in the counsel of the ungodly, Nor stand in the path of sinners, Nor sit in the seat of the scornful; But his delight is in the law of the Lord, And in His law he meditates day and night (Psalm 1:1–2).

Every time God's people violated this basic principle, catastrophe resulted.

Lot entered into an unholy alliance with Bera, king of Sodom, and as a result lost all his wealth, his position, his home, and finally his wife (Genesis 19:1–26).

Asa entered into an unholy alliance with Ben-Hadad, king of Aram, and as a result emptied both the royal and the temple treasuries, virtually bankrupting the kingdom (1 Kings 15:16–19).

Jehoshaphat entered into an unholy alliance with Ahab the apostate, king of Israel, and as a result nearly lost his life to deception and intrigue (1 Kings 22:24–33; 2 Chronicles 18:1).

Having failed to learn his lesson, Jehoshaphat entered into still another unholy alliance, this time with Ahab's son Ahaziah, and as a result, the entire royal fleet was lost in Ezion-Geber (2 Chronicles 20:35–37).

God's intention was not simply to make Israel insular and isolationist (Isaiah 56:9–12). Neither were His prohibitions an expression of prejudice (Acts 10:34). They were moral, not political. They were ethical, not cultural.

Israel was to nurture the nations of the earth (Isaiah 49:6). Israel was to be a light to the nations (Isaiah 42:6). That meant that God's people had to be a "peculiar people" (Deuteronomy 14:2). They had to be a "nation of priests" unto the Lord (Exodus 19:6). They had to be utterly uncompromised and uncompromising (Deuteronomy 18:9–13).

Otherwise, they would not be able to lead all the peoples of the earth to truth and righteousness (Matthew 15:14). They would not be able to be the "nursery of the Kingdom" (Jeremiah 5:30–31). Since dominion is accomplished through *service*, whenever they allowed evil doers to *serve* as their security, they yielded their authority and dominion to them.

Thus, if believers are "to go and make disciples of the nations, baptizing them in the name of the Father and the Son and the Holy Spirit, teaching them to observe all that (Christ has) commanded" (Matthew 28:19–20), then we *must abstain from all unholy alliances, relying solely and completely upon the Lord.*

The Nursery of the Kingdom

When the church inherited Israel's charge to nurse the nations of the earth with the waters of life (Revelation 22:17), the bread of life (John 6:31; 1 Corinthians 11:24), and the Word of life (1 John 1:1), she also inherited the prohibition against unholy alliances.

> Do not be unequally yoked together with unbelievers. For what fellowship has righteousness and lawlessness? And what communion has light with darkness? And what accord has Christ with Belial? Or what part has a believer with an unbeliever? And what agreement has the temple of God with idols? For you are the temple of the living God. As God has said: "I will dwell in them and walk among them. I will be their God, And they shall be My people. Therefore, Come out from among them and be separate," says the Lord. "Do not touch what is unclean, And I will receive you. I will be a Father to you, And you shall be My sons and daughters to Me, Says the Lord Almighty." Therefore, having these promises, beloved, let us cleanse ourselves from all filthiness of the flesh and spirit, perfecting holiness in the fear of God (2 Corinthians 6:14–7:1).

The absolute importance of this command is brought into focus, interestingly enough, in the celebration of the Lord's Supper.

The Lord's Supper! Again?

Again, indeed! As it turns out, the Lord's Supper is one of *the* primary sources of Biblical instruction on charity.

The common meal was to be protected from all defilement and trivialization: from divisions and factions (1 Corinthians 11:18–19), from selfishness and gluttony (1 Corinthians 11:21–22), from false motives and lack of commitment (1 Corinthians 11:23–25), from dry ritualism and unworthiness (1 Corinthians 11:26–27), and from self righteousness and judgmentalism (1 Corinthians 11:28–29).

The meal was to be pure and undefiled, because it was the celebration of a New Era, a New Covenant (Luke 22:20). Again, this is what Jesus was talking about when He said,

> The kings of the Gentiles exercise lordship over them, and those who exercise authority over them, are called. "benefactors." But not so among you; on the contrary, he who is greatest among you, let him be as the younger, and he who governs as he who serves. For who is greater, the one who sits at the table, or he who serves? Is it not he who sits at the table? Yet I am among you as the One who serves. But you are those who have continued with Me in My trials. And I bestow upon you a kingdom, just as My Father bestowed one upon Me, that you may eat and drink at

My table in My kingdom and sit on thrones judging the twelve tribes of Israel (Luke 22:25-30).

In the New Era, the New Covenant, Christ gathers His people around His bountiful table and feeds them. He then sets them upon thrones to judge over the Kingdom. Unlike the unbelievers who trust men and the ways of men, the servant rulers at God's table are set apart by their humble commitment to trust Christ and the ways of Christ.

Unmarked by unholy alliances and the striving of mere men, the service of the Lord's Supper was thus the ultimate sign of the church's influence over the world. It marked her dominion over the powers and principalities and it distinguished her from the so-called "benefactors" of the world. It set her apart as the nursery of the Kingdom: serving from the very table of God.

The crumbs from this spiritual table are to feed the world (Matthew 15:27).

Bureaucracies and Benefactors

The contemporary church has, in utter defiance of this basic Biblical truth, struck a deal with the "benefactors," thus diluting or perhaps even nullifying their influence over the world. Though her leaders readily acknowledge their responsibility to care for the poor, they have "gone down to Egypt" for help. Like Ahaz, they have looked around at apparently impossible circumstances and have decided to enter into an unholy alliance. Instead of trusting God, feeding the hungry, clothing the naked, sheltering the homeless, and comforting the distressed His way, from the table of the Kingdom, they have run to the lumbering bureaucracies of big government for assistance.

Scripture demands that *Christians do the work of charity, not bureaucrats.* Scripture asserts that the *church is* to be society's primary advocate for the needy, *not the state. Believers* are to lead the way with unswerving compassion and concern.

In no other way can God's people gain long-term dominion and authority. The principle of service is the foundation of dominion.

When the church and her leaders call for more government interference in the economy, more programs to "help the poor," and more legislation to provide entitlements, benefits, and affirmative action, the work of the Kingdom is inevitably compromised and paralyzed. An unholy alliance has been forged. When the church and her leaders go and ask the state to do what she should be doing, when she attempts to escape her responsibility by placing it on the shoulders of bureaucracy, dominion is subverted. When the church abandons the table of the Lord, and the responsibility to serve from that table, she also abandons her right to sit upon the thrones of judgement.

The poor must be cared for.

But it is the community of faith that must do the caring. The church is to nurse the world, not the state. The *church* must serve.

And she must do it unhindered and unencumbered by unholy alliances.

Then and only then can the church take her proper place leading, influencing, shaping, and guiding the world. Then and only then can the church "be like a watered garden, and like a spring of water whose waters do not fail" (Isaiah 58:11). Then and only then can the church "rebuild the ancient ruins" and "raise up the age-old foundations" and "be called the repairer of the breach, the restorer of the streets in which to dwell" (Isaiah 58:12).

Then and only then can the Great Commission be accomplished in any measure.

Volker's Lesson

William Volker was a millionaire back in the days when a million dollars was a lot of money. He was an immigrant who started with nothing, and he amassed a fortune. And from the first day as a youth when he went to work, he tithed. Over his lifetime, he gave away a fortune—no, several fortunes.

Volker, in 1910, as a leading citizen of St. Louis, Missouri, helped organize one of the first publicly funded welfare departments in the nation, the Municipal Department of Public Welfare. He contributed vast sums to it—the last major donor from the private sector. He had to learn the hard way that charity and authority are directly linked.

The Department was operated by the city. And through that charitable base the city's politicians laid the foundations for one of the most powerful political machines in American history. The man who inherited control of the Department was Tom Pendergast. Since he knew how to use that control politically, Pendergast was able to make and unmake politicians in Missouri for several decades, including an obscure justice of the peace named Harry Truman.

By 1918, Volker realized what his decision had really cost the city, and he vowed never again to compromise on this fundamental principle: *the separation of charity and State.* Never again would he mix charity with politics. He had learned his lesson the hard way.

Politicians always try to buy votes with tax dollars. He adopted as his goal in life Jesus' words: "Take heed that you do not do your charitable deeds before men, to be seen by them. Otherwise you have no reward from your Father in heaven" (Matthew 6: 1). From 1918 on, he did his charity in private. He gave away millions in secret. Even his biography was titled Mr. *Anonymous.* No more unholy alliances.

Conclusion

The third basic principle in the Biblical blueprint for welfare is that the church must not rely on civil government to do its job of charity. She must not even enlist the government's help. To do so would be to entangle herself in an unholy alliance.

Ahaz entangled himself and his kingdom in an unholy alliance because he simply could not bring himself to trust in the sufficiency of *God's* care. As a result, the nation was compromised and fell into terrible cycles of sin and judgement.

God wants His people to be the nursery of the Kingdom, nursing the nations of the earth on the goodness of the Word. They are to make a clear distinction between themselves and the "benefactors" of the world. The Lord's Supper illustrates that distinction: dependent disciples feeding off of God's inexhaustible bounty, serving the world, by grace through faith, this not of themselves.

Charity is too important to be left to the state. It is also way too dangerous to be left to the state.

Charity is the *church's* job, *not* the government's. Thus, individual Christians and local churches must do the job without the unholy aid of civil government.

Summary

Ahaz entered into an unholy alliance with the enemies of God and brought great suffering on his subjects, the people of Judah.

In so doing, Ahaz violated one of the most basic principles in all of Scripture: God's people must not depend on the world or the ways of the world or the men of the world; the sovereign Lord *alone is* their security.

Dominion is accomplished through *service, so* when we allow evil doers to serve as our security, we yield authority and dominion to them.

The church is charged with being the nursery of the Kingdom. Thus, the church must bring the benefits of Kingdom to the nations—not the bureaucrats, not the benefactors, but the church.

Thus when we compromise ourselves with a reliance on government to do our job, we not only yield undue authority and unwarranted dominion to them, but we also limit the effectiveness of our evangelistic impact.

Charity is too important to be left to the state. It is also way too dangerous to be left to the state. It is time we did our job.

4

HI HO, HI HO, IT'S OFF TO WORK WE GO

For even when we were with you, we commanded you this: if anyone will not work, neither shall he eat" (2 Thessalonians 3:10).

When Jesus issued a call for "laborers" for the harvest (Luke 10:2), he sure got one in Paul of Tarsus!

Paul labored in times of poverty and in times of prosperity (Philippians 4:12). He labored amidst persecution and popularity (Acts 14:8–19). He labored at home and abroad (Acts 11:25–30). He labored in season and out (2 Timothy 4:1–8). He labored with any number of friends and helpers, and he labored alone (2 Timothy 4:9–12). He continued to labor though beaten with rods, stoned, and shipwrecked (2 Corinthians 11:25). He labored on frequent journeys despite dangers from rivers, dangers from robbers, dangers from the Jews, dangers from the Gentiles, dangers in the wilderness, dangers on the sea, and dangers from false brethren (2 Corinthians 11:26). He labored through many hardships: sleepless nights, hunger, thirst, cold, and exposure (2 Corinthians 11–.27). Paul labored on and on and on.

He learned the importance of labor early in his life, long before his conversion. Though he was set aside by his education and skills to be a teacher of the Law (Acts 22:3), he still was required to learn a trade. And tentmaking was the trade he learned (Acts 18:2–3).

Tentmaking is hard work.

Later, when he began to labor for the harvest, he continued to support his ministry through tentmaking. Speaking to the Ephesian elders, he said,

Yes, you yourselves know that these hands have provided for my necessities, and for those who were with me. I have shown you in every way, by laboring like this, that you must support the weak. And remember the words of the Lord Jesus, that He said, "It is more blessed to give than to receive" (Acts 20:34–35).

He made certain to drive that same point home at every opportunity. He emphasized it when he wrote to the Corinthian church the first time (1 Corinthians 4:12, 9:14–15), and again in his second letter (2 Corinthians 11: 7, 12:13). He noted his labors twice in the first letter to the Thessalonian church (1 Thessalonians 2:9, 4:11), and again in his second letter (2 Thessalonians 3:8). And in every other New Testament letter, save one, he touched upon the issue either directly or indirectly.

In fact, one of his favorite designations for his brethren in the ministry was "co-laborer or "fellow-worker," just to make certain that the point got across (Romans 16:3, 9, 21; Philippians 2:25, 4:3; Philemon 1, 24).

The Biblical Work Ethic

The truth of it is though, Paul wasn't even all that unique among the heroes of the faith in his commitment to diligent labor. God very often used workmen, common ordinary laborers, in the enactment of his glorious plan of redemption. He used shepherds like Jacob (Genesis 30:31–43) and David (1 Samuel 17:15). He used farmers like Amos (Amos 7:14) and Gideon (Judges 6:11). He used merchants like Abraham (Genesis 13:2) and Lydia (Acts 16:14). He used craftsmen like Aquila (Acts 18:2–3) and Oholiab (Exodus 31:6). He used artists like Solomon (1 Kings 4:32) and Bezalel (Exodus 31:2–5). And the disciples He chose to convert the nations of the earth in the first century were laborers, men of low esteem: tax collectors and fishermen (Acts 4:13).

The reason for this is that work is the means by which God's people obtain their promised dominion of the earth. Eventually, the "craftsmen" will overcome the "horns" (Zechariah 1:18–21). In other words, those who work diligently at their God-ordained tasks will overcome those who grasp for power by force and deception. Notice, that throughout Scripture, implements of work are continually shown to destroy implements of war and intrigue.

Shamgar prevailed over an army of 600 Philistine warriors with only an ox goad (Judges 3:31).

Jael defeated the commander of the Canaanite army with a tent peg (Judges 4:17–22).

Gideon led his tiny band of faithful men to victory against the Midianite army with nothing more than empty pitchers, torches, and trumpets (Judges 7:13–23).

Wicked Abimelech defeated every army he marched against, but he was helpless against the millstone hurled upon his head by the woman of Thebez (Judges 9:50–54).

Samson destroyed 1,000 Philistines with nothing but the jawbone of an ass (Judges 15:14–16).

The swordless, spearless, and spiritless brigade of Saul was able to deliver Israel from the mighty Philistine army with only a small, two-man diversion (1 Samuel 13:19–14:23).

And the young David overwhelmed the giant warrior Goliath without armor, without a sword, and without shield or spear; he had only his shepherd's staff and sling, along with five smooth stones from a brook (1 Samuel 17:40–50).

Even Christ used ordinary tools, implements of work, when He made a spectacle of the powers and the principalities: He nailed them to the cross (Colossians 2:13–15)!

Dominion comes *through* service. But it comes by work. Work is the hand that plucks the golden fruit of God's very great and precious promises. Work will ultimately, inevitably overcome force and deception. The plowshare and the pruning hook will overcome the sword and the spear.

> Now it will come to pass in the latter days, That the mountain of the Lord's house shall be established on the top of the mountains, And shall be exalted above the hills; And all nations shall flow to it. Many people shall come and say, "Come, and let us go up to the mountain of the LORD, To the house of the God of Jacob; He will teach us His ways, And we shall walk in His paths." For out of Zion shall go forth the law, And the words of the Lord from Jerusalem. He shall judge between the nations, And shall rebuke many peoples; They shall beat their swords into plowshares, And their spears into pruning hooks; Nation shall not lift up sword against nation, Neither shall they learn war anymore (Isaiah 2:2–4).

God is the one who awards power, wealth, and dominion (Deuteronomy 8:18), and He awards it to laborers and diligent workers (Proverbs 10:4).

Far from being a bitter consequence of the Fall then, work is a vital aspect of God's overall purpose for man. In fact, "a man can do nothing better than find satisfaction in his work" (Ecclesiastes 2:24, 3:22).

Work is a part of God's perfect plan for all men. We were made for work. Thus, an abundance of work is a blessing. Lack of work is a curse.

Who Are the Poor?

According to Scripture, there are basically two categories of poor people. Both categories are at least partially defined in terms of *work*. There are the poor who are *denied* the opportunity to work, and there are the poor who *refuse* the opportunity to work. The early Elizabethan "Poor Laws," upon which our social policies in Western Civilization were built until recently, called these the "deserving" and the "undeserving" poor. The Bible calls them the "oppressed" and the "sluggardly" poor.

It is critical that we thoroughly comprehend this differentiation if we are to exercise Biblical charity in any measure.

The Oppressed

The oppressed are the objects of God's special care.

Happy is he who has the God of Jacob for his help, Whose hope is in the LORD his God, Who made heaven and earth, The sea, and all that is in them; Who keeps truth forever; Who executes justice for the oppressed, Who gives food to the hungry. The LORD gives freedom to the prisoners. The LORD opens the eyes of the blind; The LORD raises those who are bowed down; The LORD loves the righteous. The LORD watches over the strangers; He relieves the fatherless and the widow; But the way of the wicked He turns upside down (Psalm 146:5–9).

I will greatly praise the Lord with my mouth; Yes, I will praise Him among the multitude. For He shall stand at the right hand of the poor, To save him from those who condemn him" (Psalm 109:30–31).

I know that the LORD will maintain the cause of the afflicted, and justice for the poor (Psalm 140:12).

He sets on high those who are lowly, And those who mourn are lifted to safety. He frustrates the devices of the crafty, So that their hands cannot carry out their plans. He catches the wise in their own craftiness, And the counsel of the cunning comes quickly upon them. They meet with darkness in the daytime, And grope at noontime as in the night. But He saves the needy from the sword, From the mouth of the mighty, And from their hand. So the poor have hope, And injustice shuts her mouth (Job 5:11–16).

Lord, You have heard the desire of the humble; You will prepare their heart; You will cause Your ear to hear, To do justice to the fatherless and the oppressed, That the man of the earth may oppress no more (Psalm 10:17–18).

The Lord executes righteousness and justice for all who are oppressed (Psalm 103:6).

When Jesus began His ministry, His attentions were especially devoted to the oppressed. He dwelt among them (Luke 5:1– 11); He ate with them (Luke 5:27–32); He comforted them (Luke 12:22–34); He fed them (Luke 9:10–17); He restored them to health (Luke 5:12–16); and He ministered to them (Luke 7:18–23). When He summarized His life's work, He quoted Isaiah, saying,

The Spirit of the Lord is upon Me, because He has anointed Me to preach the gospel to the poor. He has sent Me to heal the brokenhearted, To preach deliverance to the captives And recovery of sight to the blind, to set at liberty those who are oppressed, To preach the acceptable year of the Lord (Luke 4:18–19).

And when He responded to John the Baptist's request for evidence that He was indeed the Christ, He said,

Go and tell John the things you have seen and heard: that the blind see, the lame walk, the lepers are cleansed, and the deaf hear, the dead are raised, the poor have the gospel preached to them. And blessed is he who is not offended because of Me (Luke 7:22–23).

The Sluggards

But while the oppressed are the objects of God's special care, the sluggardly are the objects of His special condemnation.

Sluggards waste opportunities (Proverbs 6:9–10), bring poverty upon themselves (Proverbs 10:4), are victims of self-inflicted bondage (Proverbs 12:24), and are unable to accomplish anything in life (Proverbs 15:19). A sluggard is prideful (Proverbs 13:4), boastful (Proverbs 10:26), lustful (Proverbs 13:4), wasteful (Proverbs 12:27), improvident (Proverbs 20:4), and lazy (Proverbs 24:30–34). He is self-deceived (Proverbs 26:16), neglectful (Ecclesiastes 10:18), unproductive (Matthew 25:26), and impatient (Hebrews 6:12). A sluggard will die for the lack of discipline, led astray by his own great folly (Proverbs 5:22–23). Though he continually makes excuses for himself (Proverbs 22:13), his laziness will consume him (Proverbs 24:30–34), paralyze him (Proverbs 26:14), and leave him hungry (Proverbs 19:15).

True Charity

There is a *clear* distinction then between the oppressed and the sluggardly. The oppressed *would* work, if only they *could*. The sluggardly *could* work, if only they *would*.

Since the only means of moving up and out of poverty, and in fact the only means of fulfilling God's purpose for our lives, is through diligent labor, the distinction between those who will work and those who won't, has *very* important implications for poverty relief.

Charity to the oppressed involves loosening "the bonds of wickedness," undoing "the bonds of the heavy burden," and letting "the oppressed go free" (Isaiah 58:6); it involves dividing bread with the hungry, bringing the homeless poor into the house, and covering the naked (Isaiah 58:7). It involves transforming poverty into productivity.

Charity to the sluggardly, on the other hand, involves *admonition* and *reproof* (2 Thessalonians 3:15; Proverbs 13:18). The compassionate and loving response to a sluggard is to *warn* him. He is to be warned of the consequences of immorality (Proverbs 5:10), of sloth (Proverbs 6:11), of deception (Proverbs 10:3), of negligence (Proverbs 10:4), of selfishness (Proverbs 11:24), of boastfulness (Proverbs 14:23), of slackfulness (Proverbs 19:15), of drunkenness (Proverbs 21:17), of gluttony (Proverbs 23:21), and of thievery (Proverbs 28:22). Charity to the sluggardly does not add to his complacency by making life increasingly easier to abuse through promiscuous entitlement programs. Instead, charity to the sluggardly equips and enables him to move *beyond* dependency, beyond entitlement.

Subsidizing sluggards is the same as *subsidizing evil*. It is *subsidizing dependence*. It is ultimately *subsidizing slavery*—moral slavery first, and then physical slavery. On the other hand, refusing to care for the oppressed is the same as *endorsing evil*. It is *endorsing injustice*. It is ultimately *endorsing slavery*—again, moral and physical.

Implementing Care

The Apostle Paul, master laborer for the Kingdom of Christ, understood all this, and thus built into the Biblical blueprint for welfare basic work requirements; requirements that ultimately made distinctions between the oppressed, or deserving poor, and the sluggardly, or undeserving poor.

> But we command you, brethren, in the name of our Lord
> Jesus Christ, that you withdraw from every brother who walks

disorderly and not according to the tradition which he received from us. For you yourselves know how you ought to follow us, for we were not disorderly among you; nor did we eat anyone's bread free of charge, but worked with labor and toil night and day, that we might not be a burden to any of you, not because we do not have the authority, but to make ourselves an example of how you should follow us. For even when we were with you, we commanded you this: If anyone will not work, neither shall he eat. For we hear that there are some who walk among you in a disorderly manner, not working at all, but are busybodies. Now those who are such we command and exhort through our Lord Jesus Christ that they work in quietness and eat their own bread. But as for you, brethren, do not grow weary in doing good. And if anyone does not obey our word in this epistle, note that person and do not keep company with him, that he may be ashamed. And yet do not count him as an enemy, but admonish him as a brother (2 Thessalonians 3:6–15).

Those who were to gather around the table of the Lord, to eat of His bounty, to benefit from His charity, were required to work. If they refused, then they forfeited access to the table.

It was that simple.

Really, it still is.

The Christian obligation to the oppressed is to remove the bonds that hinder them, not simply to administer emergency relief. The Good Samaritan task is to set them on the road to recovery. Charity involves education, job training, family counseling, youth rehabilitation, and money management as well as soup kitchens, rescue missions, and public shelters. Charity involves legal and legislative advocacy that opens up the bottom half of the free market so that the poor are not locked out of the economy. This, in addition to advocating civil rights and civil liberties.

The Christian obligation to the sluggardly is to knock away the props. The Good Samaritan task is to get them back on their own two feet. Charity involves removing crippling "entitlements." (What a horrible word: it means that sluggards are legally *entitled* to the wealth of the thrifty.) Charity means getting rid of state-run affirmative action programs, subsidies, and giveaway schemes, as well as enacting health and hygiene programs. It involves getting rid of all state legislated impediments to labor: minimum wage laws, occupational licensing restrictions, and "closed shop" union regulations. Charity involves honest, tough love. After all, accommodating sin benefits no one.

Conclusion

The fourth basic principle in the Biblical blueprint for welfare is that work is the foundation of charity. Productivity is the only cure for poverty. Productivity is the fruit of labor. Thus, labor must be the manner and the means of poverty relief.

The Apostle Paul modeled the centrality of the work ethic in his own life and ministry. He illustrated the truth that dominion is attained through work. He showed that work was essential to the call of God upon our lives. Thus, any poor who are unwilling to work have not only denied themselves the opportunity to be all God wishes them to be, they have also denied the opportunity to receive charitable relief as well.

Handouts are not Biblical. Work is.

Charity, true charity, Biblical charity, recognizes that fact, and implements it.

Summary

Work is a central theme throughout the Scriptures. It is prominent in Paul's writings as well as all of the Old Testament because work is at the heart of man's created purpose.

The Biblical work ethic is foundational to everything Scripture has to say about wealth, poverty, dominion, and charity.

Thus, the poor can be identified and defined, at least in part, by their attitudes toward work: the oppressed who are denied the opportunity to work and the sluggardly who refuse the opportunity to work.

According to Scripture, we are to show charity to *both* the oppressed and the sluggardly, but the charity we show will be different for each: relief to the oppressed, admonition to the sluggardly.

Basic to Biblical charity then, is the imperative of the Apostle Paul, "If anyone will not work, he shall not eat."

If we are to do our evangelistic duty to care for the poor, we must not fall into the trap of promiscuous giving. We must make certain that our charity adheres to the Biblical blueprint.

5

SHEAVES FOR THE PROVIDENT

Now when you reap the harvest of your land, you shall not wholly reap the corners of your field, nor shall you gather the gleanings of your harvest. And you shall not glean your vineyard, nor shall you gather every grape of your vineyard; you shall leave them for the poor and the stranger: I am the Lord your God (Leviticus 19:9–10).

The rolling Judean hills were fresh with the sights, sounds, and smells of harvest. As Naomi and her young daughter-in-law Ruth made their approach from the southeast, the contrast must have been quite stark. The land before them was rich with grain, alive with activity, and bustling with joy. The land behind them was dry, desolate, and dismal with the bitter memory of death and deprivation. The land before them was Bethlehem, the "house of bread." The land behind them was Moab, literally the place of "no bread." The land before them was the land of promise. The land behind them was the place of condemnation (Ruth 1:2, 6).

But even though Bethlehem was the land of promise for Naomi and Ruth, offering hope where there had been only despair before, they still had a number of serious problems ahead of them.

They were impoverished. They were widows. Naomi was aged and Ruth was an alien. Neither had any visible means of support.

What could they do?

Determined to take responsibility for her mother-in-law (Ruth 1:14), Ruth does the only thing she could do. She goes out to find work (Ruth 2:2). She decides to take advantage of Israel's generous "gleaners" laws.

So Ruth the Moabitess said to Naomi, "Please let me go to the field, and glean heads of grain after him in whose sight I may find favor." And she said to her, "Go, my daughter." Then she left, and went and gleaned in the field after the reapers. And she happened to come to the part of the field belonging to Boaz, who was of the family of Elimilech (Ruth 2:2–3).

According to God's Law, charity was essentially opportunity. Opportunity to work. Opportunity to labor. Opportunity to pull one's self up by the bootstraps.

And that's all Ruth wanted! She didn't need a handout. She didn't need to stand in lines, to fill out forms, to wade through bureaucratic red tape. She needed the opportunity to work.

Now behold, Boaz came from Bethlehem, and said to the reapers, "The Lord be with you!" And they answered him, "May the Lord bless you!" Then Boaz said to his servant who was in charge of the reapers, "Whose young woman is this?" So the servant who was in charge of the reapers answered and said, "It is the young Moabite woman who came back with Naomi from the country of Moab. And she said, 'Please let me glean and gather after the reapers among the sheaves. So she came and has continued from morning until now, though she rested a little in the house" (Ruth 2:4–7).

Gleaning was hard, backbreaking work. Following behind harvesters, collecting the overlooked, cast off, and leftover grain could not have been easy or pleasant for Ruth. But she was determined to live in terms of God's covenant (Ruth 1:16–17) and to move up out of destitution by working with all diligence and fervor. This determination was impressive. And it especially impressed Boaz, the owner of the field from which Ruth was gleaning.

Then Boaz said to Ruth, "You will listen, my daughter, will you not? Do not go to glean in another field; nor go from here, but stay close by my young women. Let your eyes be on the field which they reap, and go after them. Have I not commanded the young men not to touch you? And when you are thirsty, go to the vessels and drink from what the young men have drawn." Then she fell on her face, bowed down to the ground, and said to him, "Why have I found favor in your eyes, that you should take notice of me, since I am a foreigner?" And Boaz answered and said to her, "It has been fully reported to me, all that you have done for your mother-in-law since the death of your husband, and how you have left your father and your mother and the land of your birth, and have come to a people whom you did not know before. The Lord repay your work, and a full reward be given you by the Lord God of Israel, under whose wings you have come for refuge." Then she said, "Let me find favor in your sight, my lord; for you have comforted me, and have spoken kindly to your maidservant, though I am not like one of your maidservants." Now Boaz said to her at mealtime, "Come here, and eat of the bread, and dip your piece of bread in the vinegar." So she sat beside the reapers; and he passed parched grain to her; and she ate and was satisfied, and kept some back. And when she rose up to glean, Boaz commanded his young men, saying, "Let her glean even among the sheaves, and do not reproach her. Also let some grain from the bundles fall purposely for her; leave it that she may glean, and do not rebuke her." So she gleaned in the field until evening, and beat out what she had gleaned, and it was about an epah of barley. Then she took it up and went into the city, and her mother-in-law saw what she had gleaned. So she brought out and gave to her what she had kept back after she had been satisfied (Ruth 2:8–18).

Eventually, by God's grace, and by force of an unwavering faithfulness, Ruth and Naomi were raised up out of poverty. Society, under the rule of Biblical Law, gave them an opportunity and they took it.

The Opportunity Society

The gleaning laws that Ruth took advantage of in Bethlehem were an integral part of God's blueprint for welfare.

When you reap the harvest of your land, you shall not wholly reap to the corners of your field, nor shall you gather the gleanings of your harvest. And you shall not glean your vineyard, nor shall you gather every grape of your vineyard; you shall leave them for the poor and the stranger: I am the Lord your God (Leviticus 19:9–10).

"You shall not pervert justice due the stranger or the fatherless, nor take a widow's garment as a pledge. But you shall remember that you were a slave in Egypt, and that the Lord your God redeemed you from there; therefore I command you to do this thing. When you reap your harvest in your field, and forget a sheaf in the field, you shall not go back to get it; it shall be for the stranger, the fatherless, and the widow, that the Lord your God may bless you in all the work of your hands. When you beat your olive tree, you shall not go over the boughs again; it shall be for the stranger, the fatherless, and the widow. When you gather the grapes of your vineyard, you shall not glean it afterward; it shall be for the stranger, the fatherless, and the widow. And you shall remember that you were a slave in Egypt; therefore I command you to do this thing (Deuteron-omy 24:17–22).

> When you reap the harvest of your land, you shall not wholly reap the corners of your field when you reap, nor shall you gather any gleaning from your harvest. You shall leave them for the poor and for the stranger: I am the Lord your God (Leviticus 23:22).

God's opportunity society provided protection and opportunity for aliens and sojourners (Exodus 23:9), for travelers (Deuteronomy 23:24–25), for orphans and widows (Deuteronomy 24:19), and for the needy and oppressed (Leviticus 19:9–10). If they were willing to submit to the terms of God's covenant, willing to labor, willing to glean from the edges of the field and the tops of the trees, then they would be able to make it. They would be able to transform poverty into productivity.

That is *real* charity. That is *Biblical* charity.

The opportunity provided by the gleaning laws might seem to be an isolated, historical and cultural incidence, hidden away amidst all the other obscurities of the Mosaic Law Code. Actually though, gleaning is a *prominent* feature of the Biblical blueprint for welfare, spanning over 1500 years of revelation, a millennium and a half. In fact, it is *the* prominent feature.

Gleaning is the primary means of exercising charity in the Law, of course (Leviticus 19:9–10; Deuteronomy 24:17–22), but it is also the primary means in the Old Testament books of history (Ruth 2:2), and in the Prophets (1 Samuel 21:1–6). Gleaning principles also take a high profile in the Gospels (Mark 2:23), and in the New Testament Letters (2 Thessalonians 3:10).

The Confidence Factor

When David was fleeing the wrath of King Saul, the symbol of God's provision, the showbread, became for him *actual* provision.

> Then David came to Nob, to Ahimelech the priest. And Ahimelech was afraid when he met David, and said to him, "Why are you alone, and no one with you?" So David said to Ahimelech the priest, "The king has ordered me on some busi-ness, and said to me, 'Do not let anyone know anything about the business on which I send you, or what I have commanded you. And I have directed my young men to such and such a place. 'Now therefore, what do you have on hand? Give me five loaves of bread in my hand, or whatever can be found.'" And the priest answered David and said, "There is no common bread on

hand; but there is holy bread, if the young men have at least kept themselves from women," Then David answered the priest, and said to him, "Truly, women have been kept from us about three days since I came out. And the vessels of the young men are holy, and the bread is in effect common, even though it was sanctified in the vessel this day." So the priest gave him holy bread; for there was no bread there but the showbread which had been taken from before the Lord, in order to put hot bread in its place when it was taken away (1 Samuel 21:1–6).

On the surface, this incident—focusing as it does on the Sabbath Showbread—seems to have nothing whatsoever to do with gleaning, but Scripture ties the two together, making them inseparable concepts.

The Showbread was an important part of the worship of God's covenant people. It is variously called the "continual bread" (Numbers 4:7), the "sacred bread" (Hebrews 9:2), the "bread of ordering" (1 Chronicles 9:32), and the "bread of presence" (Exodus 35:13). It was an everlasting symbol (Exodus 25:30) of the "everlasting covenant for the sons of Israel" (Leviticus 24:8). It was meant to remind the people that God is man's Provider and Sustainer, that God will ever and always feed them from His bountiful table. It was a surety that God dwelt amidst His chosen and cared for them. The Showbread was a kind of visual sermon paralleling Christ's own Sermon on the Mount:

> Therefore I say to you, do not worry about your life, what you will eat or what you will drink; nor about your body, what you will put on. Is not life more than food and the body than clothing? Look at the birds of the air, for they neither sow nor reap nor gather into barns; and yet your heavenly Father feeds them. Are you not of more value than they? Which of you by worrying can add one cubit to his stature? So why do you worry about clothing? Consider the lilies of the field, how they grow: they neither toil nor spin; and yet I say to you that even Solomon in all his glory was not arrayed like one of these. Now if God so clothes the grass of the field, which today is, and tomorrow is thrown into the oven, will He not much more clothe you, O you of little faith? Therefore do not worry, saying, "What shall we eat?" or "What shall we drink?" or "What shall we wear?" For after all these things the Gentiles seek. For your heavenly Father knows that you need all these things. But seek first the kingdom of God and His righteousness, and all these things shall be added to you (Matthew 6:25–33).

Gleaning, like the Sabbath Showbread, is God's provision for man (Mark 2:27). It is evidence that all those "who are weary and heavy laden" shall have rest (Matthew 11:28). It is the promise that the land of rest (Hebrews 4:1–11), the land flowing with milk and honey (Exodus 3:8), is set aside for the oppressed, the people of the covenant, the laborers for the harvest (Matthew 5:3–16). It is evidence that indeed,

> Blessed are you poor, for yours is the kingdom of God. Blessed are you who hunger now, for you shall be filled. Blessed are you who weep now, for you shall laugh (Luke 6:20–21).

Similarly, gleaning, like the Sabbath Showbread, is testimony that God is man's Provider and Sustainer (Psalm 55:22). It is the assurance that He "who covers the heavens with clouds, who provides rain for the earth, who makes grass to grow on the mountains, who gives to the beast its food and the young ravens which cry" (Psalm 147:7–9), will *also* "gather the outcasts of Israel" (Psalm 147:2), "heal the brokenhearted" (Psalm 147:3), "support the afflicted" (Psalm 147:6), and satisfy "with the finest of the wheat" (Psalm 147:14).

The Bible, as it so often does, ties all the loose ends together, forcing us all to see the "big picture." It shows us how all the pieces of our theological jigsaw puzzle fit together into one coherent whole. It takes us beyond mere surface legality and legalism and drives us to the heart of the matter.

God's Law was never intended to be a burden upon His people.

> The law of the Lord is perfect, converting the soul; The testimony of the Lord is sure, making wise the simple; The statutes of the Lord are right, rejoicing the heart; the commandment of the Lord is pure, enlightening the eyes; The fear of the Lord is clean, enduring forever; The judgements of the Lord are true and righteous altogether. More to be desired than gold, Yea, than much fine gold; Sweeter also than honey and the honeycomb. Moreover by them Your servant is warned; And in keeping them there is great reward (Psalm 19:7–11).

God's Law was intended to provide life, liberty, and everlasting happiness. It was intended to create an atmosphere of justice, truth, and mercy. It was intended to make Israel an opportunity society.

The Land of the Free and the Home of the Brave

Were Ruth and Naomi to migrate to any major urban area in the United States today, it is highly unlikely that they would find the kind of opportunity that they did several millennium ago in Bethlehem. And *this* is supposed to be the "Land of Opportunity."

The fault for this lies not with the lawmakers, the farmers, and the landowners. Instead, the fault lies with Christians. We have all too often perpetrated doctrines and theologies that fail to integrate the faith into a comprehensive whole. By separating "spiritual" matters from "physical" matters, we make ourselves vulnerable to Christ's condemnation:

> Woe to you, scribes and Pharisees, hypocrites! For you pay tithe of mint and anise and cummin, and have neglected the weightier matters of the law: justice and mercy and faith. These you ought to have done, without leaving others undone. Blind guides, who strain out a gnat and swallow a camel (Matthew 23:23–24).

When our churches, outreaches, and ministries begin to major on minor matters, when we develop structures that fail to reflect God's providential care for His people, we certainly are no better than the Pharisees.

Conclusion

The fifth basic principle in the Biblical blueprint for welfare is that work opportunities are created through gleaning. Gleaning is the gracious provision God built into the opportunity society so that the poor could work their way up and out of the poverty trap.

Ruth was willing to labor long and hard, and thus was the recipient of charity in Israel's opportunity society. She pulled herself up by her bootstraps. She gathered in the sheaves that God had laid out for the provident.

Scripture demonstrates that the *very laws* which Ruth took advantage of are at the heart of God's message of liberty and abundance for today. God wishes to "make a way" for His people. He desires us to conform to those laws so that once again ours can be the "Land of Opportunity."

Summary

The story of Ruth and Naomi illustrates one of the most important charitable provisions that God built into Israel's society: *opportunity* based upon the work ethic.

In charity, the work ethic is evidenced in God's provision for gleaning: the poor were given opportunities to pull themselves up by their own bootstraps, by their own labor.

The *opportunity* afforded by gleaning is a concept that runs throughout the entire Bible: the Law, the Prophets, the Gospels, and the Letters all contain affirmations that the gleaning model is basic to God's program of care.

Even in the worship of God in the temple, the provision of gracious opportunity is highlighted.

Thus if we are to care for the poor in a Biblical fashion, fulfilling our evangelistic calling to wed Word and deed, we must make our nation a *"Land of Opportunity"* once again. We must integrate gleaning opportunities into every aspect of our society: in the private sector, in the marketplace, and in the church.

6

CHARITY BEGINS AT HOME

But if anyone does not provide for his own, and especially for those of his household, he has denied the faith and is worse than an unbeliever (1 Timothy 5:8).

The job was just too big for one person. Even for a person as gifted, as dynamic, as extraordinary as Moses was.

Day after day, week in and week out, from morning until evening, the children of Israel thronged around Moses. Questions. Disputes. Complaints. Concerns.

It was just too much.

Physically, emotionally, and spiritually, Moses could hardly keep up such a demanding schedule. Besides, he had other matters to attend to. He had to plan. He had to lead. He had to care for his family. He had to attend to his relationship with the Lord.

But on the other hand, he just couldn't turn away all these people, needy people, *his* people.

So when Moses' father-in-law saw all that he did for the people, he said, "What is this thing that you are doing for the people? Why do you alone sit and all the people stand before you from morning until evening?" And Moses said to his father-in-law, "Because the people come to me to inquire of God. When they have a difficulty, they come to me, and I judge between one and another; and I make known the statutes of God and His laws" (Exodus 18:14–16).

What Moses was attempting to do was quite admirable, but it was also quite foolish. He wouldn't be able to hold up long under such a tremendous strain. And Jethro, Moses' father-in-law, knew it.

So Moses' father-in-law said to him, "The thing that you do is not good. Both you and these people who are with you will surely wear yourselves out. For this thing is too much for you; you are not able to perform it by yourself. Listen now to my voice; I will give you counsel, and God will be with you; Stand before God for the people, so that you may bring the difficulties to God. And you shall teach them the statutes and the laws, and show them the way in which they must walk and the work they must do. Moreover you shall select from all the people able men, such as fear God, men of truth, hating covetousness; and place such over them to be rulers of thousands, rulers of hundreds, rulers of fifties, and rulers of tens. And let them judge the people at all times. Then it will be that every great matter they shall bring to you, but every small matter they themselves shall judge. So it will be easier for you, for they will bear the burden with you. If you do this thing, and God so commands you, then you will be able to endure, and all this people also will go to their place in peace" (Exodus 18:17–23).

Jethro didn't want to be presumptuous. He didn't want to step beyond proper bounds. After all, he *had* "heard of all that God had done for Moses and for Israel His people—that the Lord had brought Israel out of Egypt" (Exodus 18:1); he had even "rejoiced for all the good which the Lord had done" (Exodus 18:9) saying,

... Blessed be the Lord, who has delivered you out of the hand of the Egyptians and out of the hand of Pharaoh, and who has delivered the people from under the hand of the Egyptians. Now I know that the Lord is greater than all the gods; for in the very thing in which they behaved proudly, He was above them (Exodus 18:10–11).

Still, he knew that his son-in-law was terribly overburdened, and that the situation needed to be righted. So with humble hesitation and sensitivity, he suggested that Moses decentralize the administration of justice and care in Israel.

So Moses heeded the voice of his father-in-law and did all that he had said. And Moses chose able men out of all Israel, and made them heads over the people: rulers of thousands, rulers of hundreds, rulers of fifties, and rulers of tens. So they judged the people at all times; the hard cases they brought to Moses, but they judged

every small case themselves (Exodus 18:24–26).

Jethro was simply encouraging Moses to take advantage of the principle of the division of labor.

Moses may have been able to give judicious counsel based on God's direct revelation, he may have been able to dispense "perfect" justice, and he may have been able to provide instantaneous satisfaction to the people, but he was ultimately limited by time and space. And those were limitations that no amount of brilliance or inspiration could overcome.

Besides, there were literally hundreds of qualified and gifted men among the people who were not being utilized at all in the work of the ministry. They were men who feared God, men of truth, men who hated dishonest gain–men who were simply wasting their leadership capabilities (Exodus 18:21).

God's plan was to make them a "nation of priests" (Exodus 19:6). He wanted to equip them *all* to be a peculiar people (Deuteronomy 26:18), a light to the nations (Isaiah 42:6), zealous for good works (1 Peter 2:9). It would be necessary then to give them individual responsibilities. To decentralize. To effect a division of labor. To recognize the gifts and callings of the people. *All* the people.

Empire vs. Kingdom

What is the source of mankind's earthly blessings? The Bible is clear: God is. "And you shall remember the Lord your God, for it is He who gives you power to get wealth, that He may establish His covenant which He swore to your fathers, as it is this day" (Deuteronomy 8:18). "Every good gift and every perfect gift is from above, and comes down from the Father of lights, with whom there is not variation or shadow of turning" (James 1:17).

What is the proper source of earthly authority? The Bible is clear on this point: God is. God executes judgement, in time and on earth (Deuteronomy 8:19–20).

How does God exercise His authority? Both directly and indirectly. God has established several earthly institutional intermediaries (representatives), but He never relies on them exclusively. God's people can always appeal to God directly through prayer. God is the final judge. He also judges men and institutions continually. He brings continual earthly judgement.

Earthly rewards and punishments come from God. This is what pagan societies deny. They allow God to be a final judge beyond time, maybe, but He is not allowed to be a temporal judge, ever. Other judges fulfill the role of final judge in pagan societies. Other gods reward and punish. Understand: He who rewards is He who punishes. The source of charity is also the source of power. In most pagan societies historically, the state has become the final judge: the ultimate dispenser of earthly rewards and punishments.

Whenever we find a doctrine of a final earthly authority, we find ethical rebellion. We find the sin of establishing a new god: mankind.

Pagan empires are organized as top-down societies, where one man rules from on high, as if he were God Himself. This bureaucratic empire is structured like a giant pyramid. It's no wonder that the Egyptians built pyramids as symbols of their nation, with its god-pharaohs.

The Hebrews built no pyramids for themselves. They built no Babylonian pyramid-like ziggurats (stepped pyramids reaching to the sky). Their only building of importance was the Temple, and even that came almost five centuries after they fled Egypt (1 Kings 6:1). Why no pyramids? Because God's Kingdom model isn't anything like a pyramid.

The Kingdom of God is structured far differently from pagan empires. Absolute authority is always with God, and only with God. But that authority is personally applied through His Law by the Holy Spirit, and also through God-designed human institutions. Since nobody can legitimately claim to be God except God, no one can claim to be a final earthly authority. This means that the basis of the Kingdom must be a bottom-up system of multiple courts. Not one chain of command—*many.*

God deals with His people directly and personally. They can pray to Him, and He hears their prayers. No intermediary is necessary. God's people are *saints.* This means that they have direct access to God's *sanctuary* through prayer. God never establishes human institutional barriers between Himself and His people's prayers. God warns His people: "You shall not afflict any widow or fatherless child. If you afflict them in any way, and they cry at all to Me, I will surely hear their cry; and My wrath will become hot, and I will kill you with the sword; your wives shall be widows, and your children fatherless" (Exodus 22:22–24). But He *does* require intermediary institutions in order to *restrain evil men.* The three main ones are church, family, and state.

There was a brief time in Israel's history when its structure of authority did resemble an empire: the period of the exodus. Moses was in complete authority. He was their representative before the pharaoh and before God. But then God removed this empire-like system. We can date the shift in Israel's institutional structure "from empire to Kingdom" back to Jethro's wise counsel to his son-in-law, and Moses' wise concurrence.

Decentralization

Thus, the principle of decentralization that Jethro advocated was not merely a matter of convenience, effected just for the sake of Moses. It was an essential part of God's plan for His covenant people. Israel was *not* to be an empire. It was to be a decentralized Kingdom of righteousness ruled by the Sovereign Lord. This is evident throughout Scripture.

When God gave instructions for the construction of the tabernacle, the plan for the division of labor was obvious. Clans, tribes, families, and individuals all had their different tasks (Exodus 35:1–35). The extravagant complexity of the work absolutely precluded the idea that one or two or even a few might be able to complete it alone. It would take teamwork. It would take a coordination of *all* the people's gifts, resources, skills, and abilities.

Then, once the tabernacle was erected and dedicated, it was necessary to divide the various tasks of maintaining and transporting the massive structure. Again, *all* the people would need to cooperate. *All* the people would need to participate. The work would *have* to be decentralized in order for it to be accomplished. Again by clans, by tribes, and by families they were given their assignments (Numbers 3:1–4:49).

When the people entered into the land flowing with milk and honey, the land of the inheritance, again the innumerable tasks had to be accomplished that no one single man or group of men could possibly handle alone. So, the various clans, tribes, and families were given different sections of the land for which they would be responsible (Joshua 13:1–14:15). Administration was to be decentralized. Government was to be decentralized. The only centralizing factor for the people at all, in fact, was the centrality of God's Law and the commonality of their covenant bond.

Each city too, was run on the basis of the division of labor. The Levites had their tasks (Deuteronomy 18:1–22); the elders in the gate had their tasks (Ruth 4:1–17); each individual family had its tasks (Judges 19:1–30); and each family member then had his or her tasks (Proverbs 31). Decentralization was woven into the very fabric of life in Israel.

This emphasis on decentralization carried over into the establishment and administration of the early church as well. Mutual ministry and the division of labor were an essential and distinguishing characteristic of the authentic Christian community. All the believers were equipped to do the work of the ministry (Ephesians 4:12) and to exercise their own peculiar gifts (Romans 12:6). In fact, each church could only grow and build itself up in love, as each part, each member, did his own work (Ephesians 4:15–16). Tasks were divided among the elders (Hebrews 12:17), the deacons (Acts 6:1–6), the teachers (1 Corinthians 12:28), the evangelists (2 Timothy 4:5), the pastors (Ephesians 4:11), the older women (Titus 2:3–5), the young men (Titus 2:6–8), the sons and daughters (Acts 2:17), and so forth. "But the manifestation of the Spirit is given to each one for the profit of all" (1 Corinthians 12:7).

There's No Place Like Home

Decentralization is one of the two major aspects of Kingdom authority. Personalism is the other. Not only is a godly society supposed to be decentralized, it is also supposed to be personalized. Not that it is to be judged by men in terms of special favors to persons. On the contrary, God is no respecter of persons, meaning *fallen* persons (Leviticus 19:15; Deuteronomy 1:17). God respects only the Person of Jesus Christ, and this is because Christ is His son, and also the perfect human who fulfilled God's perfect Law.

What is personal in the structures of the Kingdom society is God's Law. It is to be administered without respect to persons, because only one Person deserves mankind's respect: the Author of the Law.

Perhaps the most dynamic illustration of how God planned a personalized society for His people is the way He gave emphasis and authority to the *family*. The small family unit was the basic building block of the godly society.

The *family* had the primary jurisdiction in such wide-ranging endeavors as education (Proverbs 22:6), governance (Deuteronomy 6:20–25), economics (Deuteronomy 21:17), spirituality (Ephesians 6:1–4), evangelism (1 Peter 3:1–4), and charity (1 Timothy 5:3–13).

When Nehemiah was faced with the monumental task of rebuilding the walls of Jerusalem from the rubble and rubbish at hand (Nehemiah 2:1–20), he turned to *families* (Nehemiah 3:1–32). It wasn't a government project (despite the fact that Nehemiah was governor). It wasn't coordinated by experienced contractors (despite the fact that Asaph, keeper of the king's forest, was involved). It wasn't funded by large philanthropic foundations (despite the fact that the king gave his sanction and blessing). The entire effort was executed and consecrated by *families*. Each doing its own part.

When God established a system of charity in the land to care for the orphan, the widow, the alien, the stranger, the oppressed and the dispossessed, He built it largely around the family unit. He decentralized it.

Nothing could have worked better or been more compassionate. In the years since, innumerable other systems have been tried, but none has been able to match the superior record of the family.

"God sets the lonely in families" (Psalm 68:6 NIV).

Gleaning was operated and regulated not by the magistrates of the state, not by philanthropic agencies, and not even by a local bureaucracy. It was operated and regulated by individual families under the rule of God's Law (Ruth 2:4–16). This meant that the land-owners could dispense charity unhindered and unencumbered. Accountability and flexibility were made possible. Local conditions could be taken into account, and personal attention was maximized. By thus keeping charity decentralized, deinstitutionalized, and family-centered, everyone was saved from the hassles of graft, corruption, and red tape.

Like gleaning, the interest-free loan was another aspect of Biblical charity that was operated and regulated by individual families under the rule of God's Law (Exodus 22:25–27; Leviticus 25:35–37). There was no supervision by an overarching state agency, there were no administrators, there were no forms to fill out, no lines to stand in, and there was no standardized institution to conform to. The loans were simply the means by which godly families met pressing needs with available resources, above and beyond the requirements of law or responsibility.

Of course, besides gleaning and interest-free loans, Biblical charity could also be dispensed through private giving. Obviously, this too was a function of the family, independent of any outside influence or regulation except the influence and regulation of God's Law. This was the approach the Good Samaritan took on the road to Jericho (Luke 10:30–37), and it was the impulse that motivated Barnabas and other philanthropists in the first Jerusalem church when emergency relief became necessary (Acts 4:32–37).

Charity really does begin at home! But it doesn't end there.

Notice: just because charity was not under the regulatory jurisdiction of the state did not mean that families were free to do (or not to do) whatever they pleased. Gleaning was operated and regulated by individual families *under the rule of God's Law*. Private giving was operated and regulated by individual families *under the rule of God's Law*.

A natural family, an Adamic home, is just as impotent as a tyrannical, overarching state. Centralizing charity in *fallen* family structures is just as disastrous as centralizing it in *fallen* civil structures. That is why charity in the Bible is not libertarian! It is not left to the *free* discretion of families. Charity is operated and regulated by individual families, but they are families *under the rule of God's Law*.

Under the rule of God's Law, individual families are held accountable to *particular standards* of behavior. They are held accountable to the *elders* of the faith. They are held accountable to the church, the *new Family* (Ephesians 3:15).

Charity begins at home, but not in just *any* home. Charity begins with the family at home in the house of the Lord. Thus, for instance, the alms-tithe was, like gleaning, the interest-free loan, and private giving, operated on a decentralized, family-centered basis. *But,* the families did *not* operate autonomously. Each town in Israel was required to keep a benevolence fund for emergency relief purposes. Every third year, special tithes were collected for this fund and placed under the control of the elders (Deuteronomy 14:29). Any unspent Levitical tithes were also returned to the fund, to be administered by the families of the community (Numbers 18:24). But, the *families* (plural) administered the fund *together* as a *Family* (singular).

The churches in the New Testament continued this concept of coordinated but decentralized almsgiving in order to care for the needy (Acts 4:35; 1 Corinthians 16:2; 2 Corinthians 8:1–9:15).

So, charity begins at home. It is *operated and regulated by* families. But, it is *accountable to* the families' Family.

Centralization and Collapse of Care

When we depersonalize and centralize the apparatus for charity, when we yield the responsibility to care for the poor to professional humanitarians, things inevitably turn ugly. Terribly ugly. Witness the devastating failure of America's "war on poverty."

After expenditures that exceeded $840 billion in 1993, the level of poverty was only reduced by about $200 billion. (See *The Grace Commission Report,* Green Hill Publishers, Ottawa, Illinois.) That is a rather dismal failure!

But the worst of it was not the gross waste of billions upon billions of dollars. The worst of it was the awful human waste that resulted.

Decentralized, Law-ruled, family-centered Biblical charity is personal. It is intimate. It is flexible. It is efficient. It is compassionate.

Centralized government welfare, on the other hand, is a bumbling, fumbling, uncoordinated monster. It blunders its way along, splintering families, crushing incentive, decimating pride, and foiling productivity. It naturally falls into the traps of blatant mismanagement, fiscal irresponsibility, and misapportioned authority.

Why? Because it is today an aspect of the civil government. And civil governments are inherently bureaucratic these days. They do everything "by the book." In other words, the system is innately *impersonal.*

When we depersonalize and centralize the apparatus for charity, when we yield the responsibility to care for the poor to these professional humanitarians, charity ceases to exist in any practical form.

Isn't it about time that was changed?

Isn't it about time we learned the lesson of Moses and Jethro?

Conclusion

The sixth basic principle in the Biblical blueprint for welfare is that charity must be decentralized and family-oriented in order to function properly.

Moses was faced with an almost insurmountable task in dispensing justice in Israel. He tried to do it all by himself But his father-in-law, Jethro, showed him how to utilize the natural gifts and leadership abilities in others to get the big job done: decentralize.

The family is the most dynamic example of how decentralization can work effectively and efficiently under the Law of God, especially in the area of charity. God designed the family to be flexible, accountable, compassionate, and diligent. Thus, the family was and is best able to handle the tasks of overseeing gleaning, the interest-free loan, and private giving.

Charity really does begin at home.

Summary

The story of Moses and his father-in-law Jethro clarifies one of the most fundamental differences between a godly social order and an ungodly one: a righteous culture is decentralized.

While paganism always aims at empire building, Christianity always aims at Kingdom building. Thus while the empires of evil doers have always relied on centralized authority, the Kingdom of God relies on a multiplicity of authority structures: family, church, and civil government.

The emphasis on godly decentralization is evident throughout the Scriptures and affects every task set before the believer, including charity.

Like many other social welfare tasks, charity is primarily a function of the *family*. Charity begins at home.

When we fail to recognize this truth, and try to centralize and bureaucratize the care of the poor, not only, do the suffering suffer all the more, but our evangelistic outreach falters as well.

7

UPLIFTING THE UPLIFTERS

Therefore, as we have opportunity, let us do good to all, especially to those who are of the household of faith (Galatians 6:10).

Jesus told his disciples that following his ascension to the right hand of the Father, there would be difficult times ahead for them. There would be tribulation (John 16:33), persecution (Luke 21:12), and natural calamity (Matthew 24:7). There would even be times of famine and pestilence (Matthew 24:7).

But, He told them that these events, as horrible, as heart wrenching as they would be, would also serve as an *opportunity* to spread the Gospel with great power and effect.

> Then He said to them, "Nation will rise against nation, and kingdom against kingdom. And there will be great earthquakes in various places, and famines and pestilences; and there will be fearful sights and great signs from heaven. But before all these things, they will lay their hands on you and persecute you, delivering you up to the synagogues and prisons, and you will be brought before kings and rulers for My name's sake. But it will turn out for you as an occasion for testimony" (Luke 21:10–13).

Famine and calamity, like any of the other events in nature or history, were understood by the disciples to fit into the eternal program of divine *providence* (Amos 4:6; Revelation 7:8; Romans 8:28). They knew that God possessed and controlled the "forces of nature" just as surely as He flung the cosmos into existence at the creation (Psalm 104:1–35). They knew that He exercised His power over these "forces" in direct correspondence to His relationship with the people of the covenant. When the people were obedient, then He blessed the earth with fruitful abundance (Deuteronomy 28:1–14; Isaiah

4:2; Hosea 2:21-23). But when they were rebellious, He cursed the earth with empty desolation (Deuteronomy 28:15-68; Leviticus 26:14-35). The disciples knew that God used famine and calamity throughout Israel's long tumultuous history to indicate his displeasure and to warn the people to repent (1 Kings 17:1; Haggai 1:5-11).

Thus, when famine struck Judea a short time after the church was inaugurated in the first century, none of the disciples were taken by surprise.

They knew why the famine had come.

And they knew for what purpose.

The "why?" was easy. God was judging Jerusalem for her unbelief (Matthew 23:37-38).

The "for what purpose?" was equally easy. God was providing them with an opportunity for their testimony (Luke 21:13).

Jesus had said, "By this all men will know that you are my disciples, if you have love for one another" (John 13:35).

The famine gave them the opportunity to let "all men know." It gave them the opportunity to demonstrate their love, visibly and tangibly.

> And in these days prophets came from Jerusalem to Antioch. And one of them, named Agabus, stood up and showed by the Spirit that there was going to be a great famine throughout all the world, which also happened in the days of Claudius Caesar. Then the disciples, each according to his ability, determined to send relief to the brethren living in Judea. This they also did, and sent it to the elders by the hands of Barnabas and Saul (Acts 11:27-30).

When the famine struck, they sprang into action. There was no need for long drawn out emotional appeals. They were ready, willing, and able to love, not merely "in word or in tongue, but in deed and in truth" (1 John 3:18). For the righteous man, "… will not be afraid of evil tidings; His heart is steadfast, trusting in the Lord. His heart is established; He will not be afraid, Until he sees his desire upon his enemies. He has dispersed abroad, He has given to the poor; His righteousness endures forever; His horn will be exalted with honor" (Psalm 112:7-9).

When the famine proved to be prolonged, the disciples responded with *continued* sacrifice. Writing to the Corinthians, Paul encouraged their generosity, saying,

> Moreover, brethren, we make known to you the grace of God bestowed on the churches of Macedonia: that in a great trial of affliction the abundance of their joy and their deep poverty

abounded in the riches of their liberality. For I bear witness that according to their ability, yes, and beyond their ability, they were freely willing, imploring us with much urgency that we would receive the gifts and the fellowship of the ministering to the saints. And this they did, not as we had hoped, but first gave themselves to the Lord, and then to us by the will of God. So we urged Titus, that as he had begun, so he would also complete this grace in you as well. But as you abound in everything—in faith, in speech, in knowledge, in all diligence, and in your love for us—see that you abound in this grace also (2 Corinthians 8:1–7).

But with the Corinthian believers, little encouragement was necessary.

Now concerning the ministering to the saints, it is superfluous for me to write to you; for I know your willingness, about which I boast of you to the Macedonians, that Achaia was ready a year ago; and your zeal has stirred up the majority" (2 Corinthians 9:1–2).

Thus, Paul concluded his comments, saying,

But this I say: He who sows sparingly will also reap sparingly, and he who sows bountifully will also reap bountifully. So let each one give as he purposes in his heart, not grudgingly or of necessity; for God loves a cheerful giver. And God is able to make all grace abound toward you, that you, always having all sufficiency in all things, have an abundance for every good work. As it is written: "He has dispersed abroad, He has given to the poor; His righteousness remains forever." Now may He who supplies seed to the sower, and bread for food, supply and multiply the seed you have sown and increase the fruits of your righteousness, while you are enriched in everything for all liberality, which causes thanksgiving through us to God. For the administration of this service not only supplies the needs of the saints, but also is abounding through many thanksgivings to God, while, through the proof of this ministry, they glorify God for the obedience of your confession to the gospel of Christ, and for your liberal sharing with them and all men, and by their prayer for you, who long for you because of the exceeding grace of God in you. Thanks be to God for His indescribable gift (2 Corinthians 9:6–15).

The disciples understood clearly that in the providence of God they had been given a tremendous opportunity to give evidence to the world of the power of the Gospel. For them, "love your neighbor as yourself" (James 2:8) wasn't simply a slogan. It was the authenticating mark of their faith (1 John 4:12).

Again, Paul commanded them,

Bear one another's burdens, and so fulfill the law of Christ.... Do not be deceived, God is not mocked; for whatever a man sows, that he will also reap. For he who sows to his flesh will of the flesh reap corruption, but he who sows to the Spirit will of the Spirit reap everlasting life. And let us not grow weary while doing good, for in due season we shall reap if we do not lose heart. Therefore, as we have opportunity, let us do good to all, especially to those who are of the household of faith (Galatians 6:2,7–10).

To the great aggravation of the enemies of the Gospel, the disciples did indeed bear one anothers' burdens, even in times of great hardship amidst famine conditions, so that "nor was there anyone among them who lacked" (Acts 4:34).

Facilitating Good Deeds

The early church was ready, willing, and able to "do good to all, especially to those who (were) of the household of faith" (Galatians 6:10), because their very structure—congregational, familial, and interpersonal—encouraged and even facilitated such good deeds.

Besides the elders, who were ordained to the task of teaching (Titus 1:9), guarding (Acts 20:28), and ruling (Hebrews *13:17*), the church was also served by deacons (1 Timothy 3:8–13). These men were charged with the task of caring for the physical needs of the membership. They made certain that food distribution was even and efficient (Acts 6:1–6), they cared for the special needs of the widows (Acts 6:1; 1 Timothy 5:2–16), and they took care of any basic pastoral needs that might distract the elders from their work of teaching and intercession (Acts 6:4). These deacons were to be "men of good reputation, full of the Holy Spirit and wisdom" (Acts 6:3). They were to be "reverent, not double tongued, not given to much wine, not greedy for money, holding the mystery of the faith with a pure conscience" (1 Timothy 3:8– 9). They were to be "husbands of one wife, ruling their children and their own houses well" (1 Timothy 3:12). After all, if they could not manage their own households, how could they be expected to manage the household of faith? Possible candidates for the office of deacon were to be "tested," then, if they were found to be "beyond reproach," they could begin their service (1 Timothy 3:10).

These were stern requirements and for good reason. "For those who have served well as deacons obtain for themselves a good standing and great boldness in the faith which is in Christ Jesus" (1 Timothy 3:13).

The work of the deacon, and thus the office of the deacon, was *extremely* important to the health and welfare of the church. It was not to be taken lightly. If the church could not take care of its own, then what was to be made of its claim of dominion over the whole earth? If the church could not nurse its own, how could it claim to be the nursery of the kingdom? If the church could not structure itself so that it encouraged and even facilitated good deeds, how could it possibly bear a message of glad tidings and great joy, of peace on earth and good will toward men?

Just as judgement begins with the house of God (2 Corinthians 5:10), so charity must begin with the house of God (1 Corinthians 13:1–13). In the company of the faithful, charity and its fruits *must* be evidenced.

The disciples in the early church knew this, and structured their life together accordingly. Thus, they could readily say,

> Though the fig tree may not blossom, Nor fruit be on the vines; Though the labor of the olive may fail, And the fields yield no food; Though the flock be cut off from the fold, And there be no herd in the stalls—Yet I will rejoice in the Lord, I will joy in the God of my salvation. The Lord God is my strength; He will make my feet like deer's feet, And He will make me walk on my high hills (Habakkuk 3:17–19).

The work of compassionately caring for the needy within the covenant community did not rest *solely* on the deacons' shoulders. They administered the work. They supervised it. They coordinated it. And they gave it inspiration and impetus. But charity so permeated the church's "body life" that it could not possibly be contained institutionally. The people *lived* charity. Really, that was why "there was not a needy person among them" (Acts 4:34). They *continually* bore one anothers' burdens (Galatians 6:2). And more, they were constantly stimulating each other on "to love and good deeds," not forsaking assembling together, but "encouraging one another" (Hebrews 10:24–25). Their interpersonal relationships were marked by mutual ministry and care.

The church was of course blessed with tremendous gifts. And as each one had received a special gift, they employed it "ministering it to one another, as good stewards of the manifold grace of God" (1 Peter 4:10).

> Now there are diversities of gifts, but the same Spirit. There are differences of ministries, but the same Lord. And there are diversities of activities, but it is the same God who works all in

all. But the manifestation of the Spirit is given to each one for the profit of all (1 Corinthians 12:4–7).

Some had the gift of mercy (Romans 12:8). Some had the gift of hospitality (1 Peter 4:9–10). Some had the gift of service (Romans 12:7). Some had the gift of encouragement (Acts 4:36). Some had the gift of giving (Romans 12:8). And each one was called to utilize that gift to the edification of the body. Each one was called to,

> Be kindly affectionate to one another with brotherly love, in honor giving preference to one another; not lagging in diligence, fervent in spirit, serving the Lord; rejoicing in hope, patient in tribulation, continuing steadfastly in prayer; distributing to the needs of the saints, given to hospitality (Romans 12:10–13).

Each one was called to "rejoice with those who rejoice, and weep with those who weep" (Romans 12:15). Each one was called to "associate with the humble" (Romans 12:16). Each one was called to,

> walk worthy of the calling with which you were called, with all lowliness and gentleness, with longsuffering, bearing with one another in love, endeavoring to keep the unity of the Spirit in the bond of peace (Ephesians 4:1–3).

Each one was called to "walk in love" (Ephesians 5:2), exercising whatever gift God had given,

> for the equipping of the saints for the work of ministry, for the edifying of the body of Christ; till we all come to the unity of the faith and the knowledge of the Son of God, to a perfect man, to the measure of the stature of the fullness of Christ (Ephesians 4:12–13).

Thus, both congregationally, through the office of the deacon, and interpersonally, through the mutual ministry of the saints, the church was *structured* to facilitate charity.

But that wasn't all.

The families of the church were systematically taught principles of stewardship (2 Thessalonians 3:6–15). They were discipled with an eye toward good deeds (Titus 2:2–15). They were even given jurisdictional responsibilities (1 Timothy 5:3–16). In short, the families of the church were also mobilized for charity. Their very structure was aimed at encouraging and facilitating good deeds.

Families were to prepare themselves for financial difficulty, that they might *avoid* poverty. Prevention is always better than cure (Proverbs 6:6–8). They were to train their children so that thrift, self-reliance, godliness, and diligence might protect the next generation from hardship (Proverbs 22:6). They were to care for their own: parents, children, the elderly, the sick, and the infirmed (1 Timothy 5:8). They were to exercise hospitality to the dispossessed and the stranger in need (Romans 12:13; 1 Kings 17:7–16). They were to pool their resources with other families in order to tackle large charitable projects, too monumental for any one family (Acts 4:32–35; 2 Corinthians 8:1–5).

According to a survey conducted by *U S. News and World Report,* the family now ranks 17th in the list of "institutions that affect the nation, following civil government, television, bureaucracy, newspapers, and advertising! But to the early pioneers of the Christian faith, the family ranked 1st. The church relied upon a responsible Christian family structure in order to fulfill its charitable vision.

In every way, shape, and form imaginable, the church was established in abiding love so that charity could flourish. Congregational, interpersonal, and familial structures were created so that not only would charity begin at *home,* but that charity would *begin* at home!

Changing Priorities

Somehow in the intervening years we've lost that emphasis.

We haven't had to face a famine. At least, not here in America. Our worst problem is a little unemployment.

And even at that, we've been buried under an avalanche of need. With no apparatus to deal with it.

The church has failed her widows, her orphans, her elderly, her ill and infirmed.

The church has failed to disciple young men to live lives of diligence, industry, and productivity.

The church has failed to mobilize deacons for the work they are *supposed* to do.

The church has failed to catalyze the gifts of the body for good deeds.

The church has failed to train her families for victory amidst hardship and calamity.

Instead, we've placed a heavy premium on such things as building programs and media ministries. Spiritual gifts have been harnessed for personal peace and satisfaction rather than for serving the flock.

And we wonder why our testimony seems so terribly mundane in this day of ever-increasing fascinations. Like the church in the first century, we have been given a tremendous opportunity to reach our civilization with the Gospel of Christ. God has afforded us a magnificent privilege. Unlike the church in the first century, we have not yet taken advantage of that opportunity.

But, of course, the day is not yet done. With a godly change in priorities, the people of God can begin the twenty-first century on the right track.

Conclusion

The seventh basic principle in the Biblical blueprint for welfare is that we must begin the work of charity in the company of the faithful. We must take care of our own. We must create and reinforce structures in our congregations, in our families, and in our interpersonal relationships that encourage and facilitate compassion. We must uplift the uplifters.

When famine struck Judea in the first century, the disciples were ready. They had already effectively mobilized themselves into an apparatus of care and concern. Their very structure was designated to facilitate charity. So when the crisis came, they were able to spring into action. Through the deacons, through the individual gifts within the body, and through the families, the church was able to *demonstrate* their love for one another. They were able to bear testimony to the world of the transforming power of Christ. They made certain that in the company of the faithful, there would be *no* needy persons.

If we are to achieve even a measure of the success they had in bringing the Gospel to the nations, then we too must build structures of and for charity. We too must begin our mission of love in the company of the faithful.

Summary

Jesus warned His disciples that hard times would come. But He assured them that hard times would actually *advance* the cause of the Gospel.

Hardship and privation provide God's people with a tremendous opportunity for testimony. They give us the chance to show the world that the Gospel of love really does *make a difference*, not just for the hereafter, but *here and now*.

That is why God commands us to care for the people of the covenant first. We are to demonstrate the advantage of privilege of life within the Body.

The entire structure of the church was designed around this notion: elders, deacons, spirit-gifted individuals and families the uplifters—uplifting other uplifters!

Our failure to utilize this Biblical structure to implement charity has minimized the impact of our testimony. Thus if we are to in any measure fulfill our evangelistic duty, we must return to the Scriptural pattern.

8

THE UNBROKEN CIRCLE

Now Joshua the son of Nun sent out two men from Acacia Grove to spy secretly, saying, "Go, view the land, especially Jericho." So they went, and came to the house of a harlot named Rahab, and lodged there. And it was told the king of Jericho, saying, "Behold, men have come here tonight from the children of Israel to search out the country." So the king of Jericho sent to Rahab, saying, "Bring out the men who have come to you, who have entered your house, for they have come to search out all the country." Then the woman took the two men and hid them; and she said, "Yes, the men came to me, but I did not know where they were from. And it happened as the gate was being shut that when it was dark, that the men went out. Where the men went I do not know; pursue them quickly, for you may overtake them." (But she had brought them up to the roof and hidden them with the stalks of flax, which she had laid in order on the roof.) Then the men pursued them by the road to the Jordan, to the fords. And as soon as those who pursued them had gone out, they shut the gate (Joshua 2:1–7).

She was a harlot.

An outcast even from her own people, she was especially despicable in the sight of God's covenant people.

But Rahab repented.

She put her trust in Almighty God. And by grace through faith, she was saved, she and her entire household.

Rahab didn't stop at that though. Not only did she risk her life to save the spies, not only did she create a diversion for them, but she confessed her faith in the Lord. She threw in her lot with them and Him!

So before they lay down, she came up to them on the roof, and said to the men: "I know that the Lord has given you the land, that the terror of you has fallen on us, and that all the inhabitants of the land are fainthearted because of you. For we have heard how the Lord dried up the water of the Red Sea for you when you came out of Egypt, and what you did to the two kings of the Amorites who were on the other side of the Jordan, Sihon and Og, whom you utterly destroyed. And as soon as we heard these things, our hearts melted; neither did there remain any more courage in anyone because of you, for the Lord your God, He is God in heaven above and on earth beneath" (Joshua 2:8–11).

There could be no doubt about it, Rahab was a believer. She was the most unlikely of candidates for the Kingdom of God, but by her faith (Hebrews 11:31) and by her deeds (James 2:25), she *demonstrated* the sincerity of her words. The spies were impressed. But then, Rahab went one step further still.

"Now therefore, I beg you, swear to me by the Lord, since I have shown you kindness, that you also will show kindness with my fathers house, and give me a true token, and spare my father, my mother, my brothers, my sisters, and all that they have, and deliver our lives from death." So the men answered her, "Our lives for yours, if none of you tell this business of ours. And it shall be, when the Lord has given us the land that we will deal kindly and truly with you." Then she let them down by a rope through the window, for her house was on the city wall; she dwelt on the wall. And she said to them, "Get to the mountain, lest the pursuers meet you. Hide there three days, until the pursuers have returned. Afterward you may go your way." Then the men said to her, "We will be blameless of this oath of yours which you have made us swear, unless, when we come into the land, you bind this line of scarlet cord in the window through which you let us down, and unless you bring your father, your mother, your brothers, and all your fathers' household to your own home. So it shall be that whoever goes outside the doors of your house into the street, his blood shall be on his own head, and we will be guiltless. And whoever is with you in the house, his blood shall be on our head if a hand is laid on him. And if you tell this business of ours, then we will be free from your oath which you made us swear." Then she said, "According to your words, so be it." And she sent them away, and they departed. And she bound the scarlet cord in the window. Then they departed and went to the mountain, and stayed there three days until the pursuers returned. The pursuers sought them all along the way, but did not find them (Joshua 2:12–22).

In essence, what Rahab was asking was that she and her household be included in the circle of God's covenant. The phrase she used, begging that they "deal kindly" with her, generally applied to God's covenant love with His people, or the people's bond with one another. Rahab was not just trying to make a deal. She wasn't trying to pull an "I'll-scratch-your-back-if-you-scratch mine" ploy. She was genuinely submitting herself to the God of "heaven above and earth beneath."

She had heard "of the great and marvelous works of the Lord" (Deuteronomy 2:25; 7:23, 11:25; Revelation 15:3), and she *believed* what she had heard (Romans 10:17). She then made a confession of faith (Romans 10:9), and began to do righteousness, authenticating that faith with deeds (James 1:22, 3:25). Like the children of Israel on the night of Passover, she marked her home with the scarlet emblem of God's provision (Exodus 12:7–13), and then took refuge within, waiting for the redemption of her life by God's grace (Exodus 12:21–36).

She was a believer, any way you cut it.

Later, when the walls of Jericho came a-tumblin' down, Rahab came out of her house, she and her entire household (Joshua 6:22–23) to dwell "in the midst of Israel" for the rest of her life (Joshua 6:25). From then on, she would enjoy the privileges of the covenant along with all the rest of the people, submitting to its justice, partaking of its inheritance, and resting in its security.

Rahab the harlot, though once separate from the Light and Life of the ages, "alien from the commonwealth of Israel and stranger to the covenant, having no hope and without God in the world" (Ephesians 2:12), was all at once "brought near" (Ephesians 2:13). Because of god's providential grace, and her responsive faithfulness, she and all her loved ones were "grafted in" (Romans 11:17–24), "no longer strangers and foreigners, but fellow citizens with the saints and members of God's household" (Ephesians 2:19).

But not only was she grafted into the covenant, she was ultimately grafted into the royal family of Judah (Matthew 1: 5), and the Messianic line (Ruth 4:18–22).

All this, because she was willing to submit to the terms of the covenant, the God of the covenant, and the people of the covenant.

The Sojourner in the Land

There are no racial barriers in the Kingdom of God (Galatians 3:28–29). There never have been (Psalm 87:1–7). There never will be (Isaiah 2:2–4; Micah 4:1–4). The requirements for citizenship are ethical (Psalm 15:1–5). Anyone might be admitted to the circle of the covenant if he was willing to submit to its demands, even a wretched harlot from Jericho.

There were safeguards to be sure, to protect Israel from pagan pollution, from wolves in sheep's clothing. So, for instance, there were ceremonial restrictions (Exodus 12:48–49), marital restrictions (Deuteronomy 7:1–6), and restrictions on cohabitation (Joshua 6:23). But, because the Jews themselves were at one time sojourners themselves in Egypt (Genesis 15:13; Exodus 22:21; Deuteronomy 10:19, 23:7), they were to treat the foreigners in their midst with respect and acceptance.

Whether the sojourner was a part of an entire tribe, such as the Gibeonites (Joshua 9:1–27), or one of the remnant Canaanite people, or simply an individual settler, he was to receive full justice (Exodus 22:21, 23:9; Leviticus 19:33–34). He was to share in the full inheritance of the Kingdom (Ezekiel 47:22–23). He was to be loved as a brother (Deuteronomy 10:19). He was included in the provision made for cities of refuge (Numbers 35:15; Joshua 20:9), in the charity network (Leviticus 19:10, 23:22; Deuteronomy 24:19–21), and had equality under the law (Leviticus 24:22). He was even ranked with the fatherless and the widow as being defenseless; and so the Lord Himself was his protection, judging all his oppressors (Psalm 94:6, 146:9; Jeremiah 7:6, 22:3; Ezekiel 22:7; Zechariah 7:10; Malachi 3:5).

Of course, with special privilege came special responsibility. If the sojourner was to reap the rewards of Israel's theocratic republic, then he would have to function as a responsible, obedient citizen. Like any other member of the covenant he would have to honor the Sabbath (Exodus 20:10), the Day of Atonement (Leviticus 16:29), and the Feast of Unleavened Bread (Exodus 12:19). He shared the prohibitions on eating blood (Leviticus 17:10–13), immorality (Leviticus 18:26), idolatry (Leviticus 20:2), and blasphemy (Leviticus 24:16). He came under the shelter of God's promises because he obeyed God's commands.

Nothing could stay God's hand from blessing those who honored Him, just as nothing could stay His hand from judging those who dishonored him. Thus, if the sojourner wished to share in the privileges of God's chosen people, he would have to honor God by keeping His Word.

Rahab, though she was not from the company of the faithful, came into the midst of it and submitted to God's rule, depending on His Word to live. Though not of God's household, she entered in, abiding by its standards, and thus obtained its securities. Her life and liberty could not have been had any other way. Israel was an opportunity society, but only for those who observed the "rules."

Likewise, Ruth was not from the company of the faithful. She was a Moabitess. A sojourner. But the charity of God's land of bounty and table of bounty was not closed to her. She was given the opportunity to labor, to work, to glean, because she had committed herself to the terms of the covenant, the God of the covenant, and the people of the Covenant (Ruth 1:16–17). The structures of charity in Israel, designed to take care of their own, expanded their reach to include her. Because the deeds of her mouth and works of her hands proved that she would depend on the Word of God to live, she was granted the privileges of the community of faith. She was brought into the circle of the covenant, yet the circle remained unbroken.

This gracious provision of God is illustrated time after time throughout Scripture.

The Ethiopian eunuch obtained an entrance into the covenant (Acts 8:38) because he submitted himself to the terms of the covenant (Acts 8:36–37). Cornelius, the centurion, obtained the promises of the covenant (Acts 10:44–48) because he trusted the Gospel of hope (Acts 10:22, 31, 44). Similarly, when Jesus was in the district of Tyre and Sidon, a Canaanite woman received privileges of the covenant because of her great faith.

> And behold, a woman of Canaan came from that region and cried out to Him, saying, "Have mercy on me, O Lord, Son of David! My daughter is severely demon-possessed." But He answered her not a word. And His disciples came and urged Him, saying, "Send her away, for she cries out after us." But He answered and said, "I was not sent except to the lost sheep of the house of Israel." Then she came and worshiped Him, saying, "Lord, help me!" But He answered and said, "It is not good to take the children's bread and throw it to the little dogs." And she said, 'True, Lord, yet even the little dogs eat the crumbs which fall from their masters' table." Then Jesus answered and said to her, "O woman how great is your faith! Let it be to you as you desire." And her daughter was healed from that very hour (Matthew 15:22–28).

Just as the Gospel "is the power of God to salvation for everyone who believes, for the Jews first and also for the Greek" (Romans 1:16), so the privileges of the covenant are available to everyone who submits, to the household of God first, but then also to the sojourner.

Pearls Before Swine

Jesus warned his disciples about sidestepping the boundaries of the covenant, saying,

Do not give what is holy to the dogs; nor cast your pearls before swine, lest they trample them under their feet, and turn and tear you in pieces (Matthew 7:6).

The church is to be the nursery of the Kingdom, nurturing the nations on the goodness of God's bounty, but in order to taste of that goodness, the nations must submit to God's rule (Matthew 28:19–20). To dispense the gifts of the Kingdom as an entitlement to any and all men without obligation: the ungrateful, the slothful, the degenerate, the apostate, and the rebellious, is to cast our pearls before swine!

Rahab had to demonstrate her faithfulness and her integrity. She had to display fruits of repentance. Only then was she allowed to taste the inheritance of the company of the faithful.

Ruth had to work. She had to glean. She had to show her dependence on the Word of God for her very life. Only then was she allowed to reap the benefits of the opportunity society.

Similarly, the Ethiopian eunuch, Cornelius the centurion, and the Canaanite woman all received special blessing from the Lord because they demonstrated special dependence on the Lord.

In every case, all those who received the benefits of the covenant were either in the covenant (in the company of the faithful) or dependent on the covenant (the sojourner in the land).

Whenever someone violated God's standards he lost his covenant privileges: Esau (Genesis 25:27–34), Korah (Numbers 16:1–35), Achan (Joshua 7:1–26), Saul (1 Samuel 13:5–14), Tobiah (Nehemiah 13:4–9), Ananias and Sapphira (Acts 5:1–11), Demas (2 Timothy 4:10), and Diotrephes (3 John 9). There was no entitlement. God did not promiscuously hand out the privileges of the Kingdom.

Beyond Entitlement

God has exercised compassion, comfort, and charity on His people. He has fed them from His rich estate! They then have been commissioned to nurse the world with similar compassion, comfort, and charity. They are to feed the world. Beginning with their own house, they are to make certain that righteousness is *done* as well as preached.

But, charity is not to be dispensed as an entitlement, a right, bearing with it no responsibilities or obligations.

Work is required because work is the means by which poverty is transformed into productivity.

Diligence is required because diligence is blessed with prosperity.

Family participation is required because families are the basic building blocks of society.

Even more than these, though, *obedience is* required. *Submission* to the standards of the Kingdom is required. In order to take advantage of the covenant privileges, a man must be *in* the covenant or dependent *on* the covenant. Even when the church reaches out into the streets, and lanes, and hedgerows, drawing in the castoffs and dregs of the land, responsibility must be enforced.

Jesus said,

> ..."When you give a dinner or a supper, do not ask your friends, your brothers, your relatives, nor your rich neighbors, lest they also invite you in back, and you be repaid. But when you give a feast, invite the poor, the maimed, the lame, the blind. And you will be blessed, because they cannot repay you; for you shall be repaid at the resurrection of the just." Now when one of those who sat at the table with Him heard these things, he said to Him, "Blessed is he who shall eat bread in the kingdom of God!" Then He said to him, "A certain man gave a great supper and invited many" and sent his servant at supper time to say to those who were invited, "Come, for all things are now ready." But they all with one accord began to make excuses. The first one said to him, "I have bought a piece of ground, and I must go and see it. I ask you to have me excused." And another one said, "I have bought five yoke of oxen, and I am going to test them. I ask you to have me excused." Still another said, "I have married a wife, and therefore I cannot come." So that servant came and reported these things to his master. Then the master of the house, being angry, said to his servant, "Go out quickly into the streets and lanes of the city, and bring in here the poor and the maimed and the lame and the blind." And the servant said, "Master, it is done as you commanded, and still there is room." Then the master said to the servant, "Go out into the highways and the hedges, and compel them to come in, that my house may be filled. For I say to you that none of those men who were invited shall taste of my supper" (Luke 14:12–25).

The poor are to be brought in. They are to take their place around the table of the Lord. Those who refuse the invitation remain hungry outside the circle of hope, but those who accept can come in and feast with the people of hope.

But, as Matthew points out in a parallel passage, the dinner is not without obligation. The covenant must be submitted to.

> But when the king came in to see the guests, he saw a man there who did not have on a wedding garment, So he said to him, "Friend, how did you come in here without a wedding garment?" And he was speechless. Then the king said to the servants, "Bind him hand and foot, take him away, and cast him into the outer darkness; there will be weeping and gnashing of teeth." For many are called, but few are chosen (Matthew 22:11–14).

Pearls must not be cast before swine. Those who refuse to come under the rule of God after they have been taught the Gospel *can* not, and *must* not come under the protection and provision of God.

Conclusion

The eighth basic principle in the Biblical blueprint for welfare is that only those who are either *in* God's covenant or are dependent *on* God's covenant may receive charity. The work of charity begins in the company of the faithful, but it then extends to the four corners of the earth, to all who will submit to God's Word.

Rahab brought herself under the rule of God's people and God's Law and thus inherited the full security and blessings of Israel. She was grafted in, as were Ruth, the Ethiopian eunuch, Cornelius the centurion, and the Canaanite woman from Tyre. All were from outside the covenant, but made themselves dependent on it. But in order to receive its benefits they had to accept certain responsibilities. They took on certain obligations.

Pearls must not be cast before swine. The marvels of God's blessing must not be tossed out as so many baubles before the enemies of the Kingdom. Thus, if any would "taste and see that the Lord is good" (Psalm 34:8), they must first bow down before Him, and love and adore Him.

The blessings and privileges of God's children remain within the circle of the covenant. And the circle must remain unbroken.

Summary

Rahab was *not* within the covenant, but by faith she submitted herself to the demands of the covenant and thus became an heir to the blessings of the covenant. She came in by faith.

That is the only way she *could* have received the blessings of the covenant, because they are *directly* tied to the ethical and moral demands of God.

Whenever anyone receives the blessings of God, they must do as she did: submit to the moral requirements of the Kingdom. God is gracious, but He is not promiscuous.

Since we must not cast pearls before swine, we must be careful not to cast the blessings and privileges of the covenant before those who obstinately refuse to follow God's "rules."

This means that in charitable ministry to the poor we must move beyond "rights" and "entitlements" to Biblical obligations and responsibilities. Those who refuse to come under the rule of God, after they have been taught their covenant obligations, *cannot* come under His protection either.

9

EXCEEDING WHAT IS WRITTEN

... It came to pass in the month of Chislev, in the twentieth year, as I was in Shushan the citadel, that Hanani one of my brethren came with men from Judah; and I asked them concerning the Jews who had escaped, who had survived the captivity, and concerning Jerusalem. And they said to me, "The survivors who are left from the captivity in the province are there in great distress and reproach. The wall of Jerusalem is also broken down, and its gates are burned with fire." So it was, when I heard these words, that I sat down and wept, and mourned for many days ... (Nehemiah 1:1–4).

The news utterly devastated him. He was a man of high station, of great privilege. He dwelt in the lap of luxury amidst the marvelous splendor of palace life.

He was far, far removed from the world of deprivation, devastation, and destruction. He was far from the grief, the humiliation, and the shame that was Jerusalem's.

Yet, it was all driven home to him as he heard the news. Nehemiah, son of Hacaliah, cupbearer to the Persian monarch, Artaxerxes, was still, very much, a man of his people.

Something had to be done. The situation was intolerable as it was.

Nehemiah was a man of influence. He was a man of action. Perhaps he could do something.

So he did.

I was fasting and praying before the God of heaven. And I said: "I pray, Lord God of heaven, O great and awesome God, You who keep Your covenant and mercy with those who love You and observe Your commandments, please let Your ear now be attentive and Your eyes open, that You may hear the prayer of Your servant which I pray before You now, day and night, for the children of Israel Your servants, and confess the sins of the children of Israel which we have sinned against You. Both my father's house and I have sinned. We have acted very corruptly against You, and have not kept the commandments, the statutes, nor the ordinances which You commanded Your servant Moses. Remember, I pray, the word that You commanded Your servant Moses, saying, "If you are unfaithful, I will scatter you among the nations, but if you return to Me, and keep My commandments and do them, though some of you were cast out to the farthest part of the heavens, yet I will gather them from there, and bring them to the place which I have chosen as a dwelling for My name. "Now these are Your servants and Your people, whom You have redeemed by Your great power, and by Your strong hand. O Lord, I pray, please let Your ear be attentive to the prayer of Your servant, and to the prayer of Your servants who desire to fear Your name; and let Your servant prosper this day, I pray, and grant him mercy in the sight of this man." For I was the King's cupbearer (Nehemiah 1:4–11).

He did something, all right.

He prayed.

He prayed a prayer of confession. He prayed a prayer of contrition. Instead of immediately charging into the throne room of Artaxerxes and demanding attention, he immediately fell to his knees before God upon His throne and admitted his inability and inadequacy to *demand* anything.

He prayed.

He knew ultimately he was going to have to remedy the situation in Jerusalem, and that in order to do that he would have to win the king's favor (Nehemiah 1:11).

But for now He just prayed.

For an entire month he prayed (Nehemiah 1:1, 2:1).

His response speaks volumes for his character and for the character of his faith. He understood clearly the consequences of sin (Jeremiah 14:1–22). He had a good grasp of the dynamics of history (Job 42:1–2). He showed a thorough understanding of the doctrine of divine providence (Proverbs 21:1). He obviously comprehended the multigenerational nature of the covenant bond (Lamentations 5:19). He displayed a keen awareness of the power of prayer (2 Chronicles 7:13–14). But more than anything else, his response gives testimony to his utter dependence upon God, and his confidence in *Biblical* problem solving (Psalm 34:17–18). He wanted to do things God's way, in God's time, with God's help, in accord with God's will.

So, at every turn, Nehemiah prayed. When he appeared before the king to make petition to rebuild the walls of Jerusalem, he prayed (Nehemiah 2:4). When he entered into the ruined city to begin the task, he prayed (Nehemiah 2:12). When threats of violence and conspiracy jeopardized the fledgling reconstruction project, he prayed (Nehemiah 4:2). When there were crises among the people that required his judicious hand, he prayed (Nehemiah 5:19). When an attempt on his life threatened the entire project, he didn't panic—he prayed (Nehemiah 6:9). When his own brethren turned against him, he prayed (Nehemiah 6:14). And when he completed the work, all that he had set his hand to do—that's right; you guessed it—he prayed (Nehemiah 13:31).

Of course, praying wasn't *all* that he did. It was simply the *foundation* of all that he did. He planned (Nehemiah 2:5–6). He laid groundwork (Nehemiah 2:7–8). He enlisted help (Nehemiah 2:9). He encouraged (Nehemiah 2:17–18). He motivated (Nehemiah 4:14–20). He organized (Nehemiah 3:1–32). He anticipated difficulty and made provision for it (Nehemiah 2:19–20, 6:1–14). He improvised (Nehemiah 4:21–23). He worked Nehemiah 4:23). He sacrificed (Nehemiah 5:14–19). He led (Nehemiah 13:4–30). And he governed (Nehemiah 7:1–7). But undergirding all these activities was his constant reliance upon Almighty God. Undergirding them all was prayer.

Nehemiah knew that it was pointless to attempt anything apart from God's blessing and purpose.

> "Unless the Lord builds the house, They labor in vain who build it; Unless the Lord guards the city, The watchman stays awake in vain. It is vain for you to rise up early, To sit up late, To eat the bread of sorrows; For so He gives to His beloved sleep" (Psalm 127:1–2).

The prayer life of Nehemiah pointed to the fact that he wanted to be accountable. Accountable for his actions. Accountable for his intentions. Accountable for the fruit of his labor. Accountable to God. He wanted more than anything else to do God's will.

He had no desire to have God simply "okay" his plans. He wanted to do what *God* wanted him to do, nothing more and nothing less. Prayer held him accountable to that. It gave him the resolve to *stick* to that. Prayer gave him access to God's will, God's way, God's purposes, and God's plan.

Nehemiah was *confident* that God would give him success (Nehemiah 2:20). He was *sure* that God would give him strength (Nehemiah 6:9). He *knew* that God would give him favor (Nehemiah 2:18). He was, in fact, absolutely unwavering in his optimism, because the work was conceived by God, not by him (Nehemiah 2:12). It was God's project, not his (Nehemiah 7:5).

Nehemiah didn't pray in order to *get* something. He prayed in order to *be* something (James 4:3). He wanted to *be* conformed to God's will. He wanted to *be* used in God's work. He wanted to *be* obedient.

Prayerful Obedience

Nehemiah's conformity to God's purposes is evidenced not only in his prayer life, but in his emphasis on the Scriptures as well. In fact, his prayer life ultimately led him to the Word with renewed commitment. Because he so desired to do only the will of God, and because the Bible is the written and revealed will of God, it was only natural that Nehemiah's prayer life would be inextricably tied to Scripture.

He gave prominent place to the work of God's Law in the life of the people (Nehemiah 8:1–8). He gave the Bible proper perspective (Nehemiah 8:9) and appropriate priority (Nehemiah 5:1–3). He encouraged its reading (Nehemiah 8:18), its exposition (Nehemiah 8:13), and its application (Nehemiah 8:14–18). He made certain that God's Word became the absolute standard for worship (Nehemiah 13:10–14), for commerce (Nehemiah 13:15–18), for governance (Nehemiah 13:4–9), for administrating justice (Nehemiah 13:19–22), and for family life (Nehemiah 13:23–29).

He knew that to conform himself to God's will he would have to pay heed to the eternal, established Word of Truth (Psalm 119:152).

The grass withers, the flower fades, But the Word of our God stands forever (Isaiah 40:8).

"For My thoughts are not your thoughts, Nor are your ways My ways," says the Lord. "For as the heavens are higher than the earth, So are My ways higher than your ways, And My thoughts than your thoughts. For as the rain came down, and the snow came down from heaven, And do not return there, But water the earth, And make it bring forth and bud, That it may give seed to the sower And bread to the eater, So shall My Word be that goes forth from My mouth; It shall not return to me void, But it shall accomplish what I please, And it shall prosper in the thing for which I sent it" (Isaiah 55:8–11).

This Book of the Law shall not depart from your mouth, but you shall meditate in it day and night, that you may observe to do according to all that is written in it. For then you will make your way prosperous, and then you will have good success (Joshua 1:8).

The Law of the Lord is perfect, converting the soul; The testimony of the Lord is sure, making wise the simple (Psalm 19:7).

Nehemiah prayed so that he might not fall into error. And he diligently applied himself to Scripture for the same reason (Matthew 22:29), for the Word gives perfect guidance into all truth (Psalm 119:160). It is a lamp to the feet and a light to the path (Psalm 119:105).

The entrance of Your words gives light; It gives understanding to the simple (Psalm 119:130).

For the commandment is a lamp, and the Law is light; Reproofs of instruction are the way of life" (Proverbs 6:23).

We also have the prophetic word made more sure, which you do well to heed as a light that shines in a dark place, until the day dawns and the morning star rises in your heart; knowing this first, that no prophecy of Scripture is of any private interpretation, for prophecy never came by the will of man, but holy men of God spoke as they were moved by the Holy Spirit (2 Peter 1:19–21).

All Scripture is given by inspiration of God, and is profitable for doctrine, for reproof, for correction, for instruction in righteousness, that the man of God may be complete, thoroughly equipped for every good work (2 Timothy 3:16–17).

To go *beyond* Scripture would have meant to evade the purposes of God (1 Corinthians 4:6). The more Nehemiah drew near to God in prayer, the more he depended on Him for guidance, the more he realized that Scripture was the *only* rule he needed for life and godliness. God's will was to be found in God's Word. God Himself was clear enough on that score:

You shall not add to the Word which I command you, nor take anything from it, that you may keep the commandments of the Lord your God which I command you (Deuteronomy 4:2).

Whatever I command you, be careful to observe it; you shall not add to it nor take way from it (Deuteronomy 12:32).

Every Word of God is pure; He is a shield to those who put their trust in Him. Do not add to His words, Lest He reprove you, and you be found a liar (Proverbs 30:5–6).

Diligence in prayer *always* drives God's people to dependence on the Word. Nehemiah was not a solitary example. Such was the case with David (Psalm 51:1–19), and Jeremiah (Lamentations 5:1–22), and Jonah (Jonah 2:2–9), and the disciples (Acts 1:8–14), and the Jerusalem church (Acts 2:1–47).

Likewise, a failure to seek God in fellowship leads invariably to a violation of God's Word and a rejection of His purposes. Such was the case with Cain (Genesis 4:3–8), and Korah (Numbers 16:1–35), and Balaam (Numbers 22:2–40), and Saul (1 Samuel 13:5–14).

Obedience and Poverty Relief

The only cure for poverty is *productivity.* A transfer of wealth won't do it. Simpler life styles won't do it. Better laws won't do it. More government programs won't do it. Only productivity will do it. And the only means for attaining productivity is through obedience and diligence.

God blesses obedience with prosperity (Deuteronomy 28:1–14, 7:12–26, 11:13; Exodus 15:26, 23:22–27; Leviticus 26:3–13).

Likewise, God blesses diligent labor with dominion (Proverbs 10:4, 12:11–12, 22:29, 28:19; Zechariah 1:18– 20).

Nothing else works. *Nothing.*

That is why most poverty programs have failed so miserably, including socialism's "war on poverty."

They have tried to *supplement* Biblical teaching. Or, they have tried to *supplant* Biblical teaching. Or, they have tried to *supersede* Biblical teaching. Or, they have tried to *sidestep* Biblical teaching. Whatever, and however, they have failed.

They have failed because they refused to submit to God's standards. They have not been accountable to Him. They have not been dependent on Him. They have not striven for productivity through obedience and diligence. They have not *sought* Him to discover and do His will.

There are even a number of prominent Christians in our day who assert that there is no economic system that is inherently Christian in nature. They argue that there are no Biblical blueprints for charity. To their mind, God has no specific plan; He simply has vague "concerns" to be addressed through vague "principles."

Unlike Nehemiah, these men feel no obligation to humble themselves before Almighty God, making certain "not to exceed what is written" (1 Corinthians 4:6). Instead, they plunge ahead in the grips of guilt and pity, the two faces of the church's own "Janus monster." They plunge ahead to "help the poor." Impulsively. Hastily. Doing what is right in their own eyes (Judges 21:25).

And they wonder why they fail!

Nehemiah could have told them.

> Every way of a man is right in his own eyes, But the Lord weighs the hearts. To do righteousness and justice is more acceptable to the Lord than sacrifice.... The plans of the diligent lead surely to plenty, But those of everyone who is hasty, surely to poverty (Proverbs 21:2–3, 5).

Poverty "relief" programs always lead to *more* poverty, unless they seek and do God's will.

Thus diligent prayer and strict obedience to Scripture will mark any successful charity outreach.

> So He humbled you, allowed you to hunger, and fed you with manna which you did not know nor did your fathers know, that He might make you know that man shall not live by bread alone; but man lives by every Word that proceeds from the mouth of the Lord (Deuteronomy 8:3).

> Therefore, laying aside all malice, all guile, hypocrisy, envy, and all evil speaking, as newborn babes, desire the pure milk of the Word, that you may grow thereby (1 Peter 2:1–2).

Accountability to God is far more important than resources, facilities, political connections, media support, community cooperation, professional expertise, social acceptability, or cultural clout. After all, "if God is for us, who can be against us?" (Romans 8:31).

Conclusion

The ninth basic principle in the Biblical blueprint for welfare is that charity must not "exceed what is written." It must be rooted in prayerful dependence upon God and God's Word. It must seek *His* will, *His* agenda, and *His* purposes.

Nehemiah was a man who demonstrated his total dependence on God. He was a man of prayer. He was a man of the Word. As a result, in every endeavor, he sought to do the *work* of the Lord, in the *way* of the Lord. "Not my will, but thine" might very well have been his motto. As a result, God blessed him with *great* success. He refused to "exceed what is written" (1 Corinthians 4:6), and thus he never stepped beyond the bounds of God's purposes.

Summary

Nehemiah was a man of prayer. He looked to God and to God alone for his direction.

He was also a man of the Word. He knew that it was essential to the success of any endeavor to operate within the limits set by Scripture.

God tells us what to do, when, where, how, and why. To follow any other course than the course God has set for us insures utter failure. Nehemiah understood that.

Unfortunately, most of our efforts on behalf of the poor are entirely uninspired. They exceed what is written, or they fall short of what is written, or they ignore what is written. And so they fail.

Poverty "relief" programs *always* lead to *more* poverty unless they seek and do God's will. Thus in order to be effective, our charity outreaches must be marked by diligent prayer and strict obedience to Scripture.

No matter what task we undertake, Nehemiah's example is instructive. We must not add to, or take away from, God's revelation (Deuteronomy 4:2; Proverbs 30:6; Revelation 22:18–19). God has given us His blueprints. Let's just follow the plan. Nothing more. Nothing less.

10

THE FOUNDATION OF PEACE

"There is no peace," says the Lord, "for the wicked" (Isaiah 48:22, 57:21).

With that booming phrase, the great evangelical prophet Isaiah punctuated his final series of sermons to his beloved people, the citizens of Judah.

And what a phrase!

With a remarkable economy of words, Isaiah was able to capture the essence of his concerns. He was able to summarize his life's message. He was able to outline his theology. He was able to illustrate with absolute clarity the spiritual emphasis of his entire ministry.

All that, in one phrase.

Isaiah had dedicated himself to proclaiming to the people God's eternal purposes for them. He was forever announcing God's promises to them. He was a diligent bearer of the glad tidings of peace. God had established a "covenant of peace" with the people (Isaiah 54:10). And it was an irrevocable, everlasting covenant (Isaiah 61:8). Thus, they would be at peace with the nations (Isaiah 26:12) and at peace with God (Isaiah 27:5). They would have "peace like a river" (Isaiah 66:12) and peace "like the waves of the sea (Isaiah 48:18). There would be "peace to him who is far off and to him who is near" (Isaiah 57:19). It would be a "perfect peace" (Isaiah 26:3) wrought by the "Prince of Peace" (Isaiah 9:6).

But, Isaiah was quick to add, this great and glorious peace would only come upon *God's faithful* covenant people. "There is no peace for the wicked" (Isaiah 48:22). And sadly, as Isaiah uttered this phrase, the citizens of Judah appeared to be anything *but* God's faithful covenant people. They were treading the darksome path of wickedness.

Their worship had deteriorated into meaningless ritual (Isaiah 1:11–15). They had become proud and complacent (Isaiah 32:10). They had entangled themselves in unholy alliances (Isaiah 30:1–3). Their hearts were inclined to "iniquity: To practice ungodliness, to utter error against the Lord, To keep the hungry unsatisfied, And he will cause the drink of the thirsty to fail" (Isaiah 32:6). They were flirting with disaster (Isaiah 5:13–17). For, "There is no peace for the wicked" (Isaiah 48:22).

Thus the God of peace commanded the prophet of peace to reiterate, once and for all, the *program* for peace, saying,

> Cry aloud, spare not; Lift up your voice like a trumpet; Tell My people their transgression, And the house of Jacob their sins.... Is this not the fast that I have chosen: To loose the bonds of wickedness, To undo the heavy burdens, To let the oppressed go free, And that you break every yoke? Is it not to share your bread with the hungry, And that you bring to your house the poor who are cast out; When you see the naked, that you cover him, And not hide yourself from your own flesh? Then your light shall break forth like the morning, Your healing shall spring forth speedily, And your righteousness shall go before you; The glory of the Lord shall be your rear guard. Then you shall call and the Lord will answer; You shall cry, and He will say, "Here I am." If you take away the yoke from your midst, The pointing of the finger and speaking wickedness, If you extend your soul to the hungry, And satisfy the afflicted soul, Then your light shall dawn in the darkness, And your darkness shall be as the noonday. The Lord will guide you continually, And satisfy your soul in drought, And strengthen your bones; You shall be like a watered garden, And like a spring of water, whose waters do not fail. Those from among you shall build the old waste places; You shall be called the repairer of the breach, the restorer of streets to dwell in (Isaiah 58:1, 6–12).

Did the people want peace, perfect peace, the peace that surpasses all understanding? Did they want to reconstruct their culture, restore the foundations, and reclaim their lost legacy? Then they would have to *repent of* their wickedness and do the works of righteousness. They would have to show forth the *fruits* of grace. They would have to uphold their covenant responsibility. They would have to do their job. And clearly, charity was to be one of their *prime* priorities.

Changing the World

Charity is rather like a lever. You can move a large, heavy object if you have a lever. But you also need a fulcrum. That's the Gospel, the foundation. You need them both. With both, you can move the hearts of men, if the Holy Spirit blesses your efforts. You can even move the world, if the Holy Spirit blesses your efforts. You can usher in the peace that surpasses all understanding.

Consider Isaiah's message: if you want the peace of God, you must *demonstrate* your commitment to Him. The way He wanted them to demonstrate their commitment was by showing *charity.*

Even though the people sought the Lord "day by day," delighting to know His ways, submitting to the ordinances of the Word, and seeking His standard of justice (Isaiah 58:2), they had fallen short. Their prayers and fasting went unnoticed (Isaiah 58:3). Their humble worship went for naught (Isaiah 58:3–5). They had fallen short simply because they hadn't started at the start. Real peace, real reconstruction, and real restoration in the land would occur only if they *began* with charity to the poor and needy.

That's where God wants His people to *start.* He wants them to loosen the bonds of wickedness and to let the oppressed go free (Isaiah 58:6). He wants them to feed the hungry, shelter the homeless, clothe the naked, and comfort the distressed (Isaiah 58:7). *Then* cultural resurgence will occur. *Then* revival will blossom. *Then* God would turn the land into a garden like Eden (Isaiah 58:8–12). *Then* there would be peace.

Poverty relief isn't the *only* thing in the program for peace. It is just the *first* thing. Because poverty relief is the *first* sign, the initial mark of faithfulness to the call of God. True *revival* is rooted in compassion toward the poor and dispossessed (Luke 3:2–18). Charity is in fact at the very heart of the Gospel call (Luke 4:18).

Cultural renaissance depends upon it (Isaiah 58:12). Even final and ultimate judgement is gauged by it (Matthew 25:31–46). "Righteousness is sown in peace by those who make peace" (James 3:18).

"Now, wait a minute here," you may be saying to yourself, "I thought that *evangelism is* what would usher in peace. Or maybe *discipleship.* Certainly not *charity,* though."

The point that Isaiah makes is that charity is the *starting place* for evangelism. It is where discipleship *begins.* It is *the foundation* of peace.

When a missionary goes to a new mission field, what is the first thing he must do? His objective of course is to win souls, to make known the "Peace" of Christ Jesus, but first he must win the right to

be heard. He must exercise charity! He provides the people with
medical care, food, shelter, clothing, pure water sources, and proper
sanitation and hygiene. He wins the confidence of his hearers and
thus wins a hearing. Then, and only then, can he win souls and
make for peace (Romans 10:17).

So, charity is evangelism. It is discipleship. Or at least it is the
foundation for these tasks. Charity does not *replace* preaching, teaching, or witnessing; instead it lays the groundwork for those Gospel
tasks. Charity tills the soil so that it will be ready for and receptive to
the seeds of salvation.

The people in Isaiah's day had proven by their lack of charity,
and by their lack of righteous deeds, that they were indeed a faithless people. Their sure and secure foundations were thus shaken and
their peaceful inheritance was jeopardized.

Still, God beckoned to them. Though they refused to honor the
terms of the covenant, God's pledge to them was everlasting and
irrevocable (Isaiah 55:3). He prodded them through His servant Isaiah to turn about and do right, saying,

> "Wash yourselves, make yourselves clean; Put away the evil
> of your doings from before My eyes. Cease to do evil, Learn to do
> good; Seek justice, Reprove the oppressor; Defend the fatherless,
> Plead for the widow. Come now, and let us reason together," Says
> the Lord, "Though your sins are like scarlet, They shall be as
> white as snow; Though they are red like crimson, They shall be
> as wool. If you are willing and obedient, You will eat the good of
> the land; But if you refuse and rebel, You shall be devoured by
> the sword. For the mouth of the LORD has spoken (Isaiah 1:16–
> 20)."

The message came through loud and clear. There would never
be any peace, though peace was their rightful inheritance, until
they made charity a central priority. The peace that would make
them like a watered garden, lit by the glories of the Lord, guarded by
His very righteousness, graced by His very presence, like the garden
of Eden (Isaiah 58:8–12) could not be attained until they gave themselves to the hungry, and satisfied the desire of the afflicted (Isaiah
58:10).

Notice again the emphasis here. Charity is not a peripheral
matter. It is not a side issue. It is not secondary to other concerns. It
is not something that believers can get around to when they jolly
well please. Indeed, "This is pure and undefiled religion in the sight
of our God and Father, to visit orphans and widows in their distress,
and to keep oneself unstained by the world" (James 1:27).

From Here to There

At a time when global thermonuclear war is an all too real possibility, we all know the *urgency* of peacemaking. But, dominion doesn't happen overnight. Peace isn't won in a day.

Even at Jericho, when God miraculously delivered the city into the hands of His people, they had to march around the walls for days on end. They had to wait.

Dominion is a multigenerational task. It takes time. It takes work.

Jonathan knew that. So he went to work immediately. He understood the urgency of the situation, so he acted boldly. He knew that the restraints of time demanded decisiveness.

Israel was laboring under the terrible bondage of the Philistines. The army of Jonathan's father, Saul, was defenseless and demoralized, owning no swords, and no spears!

> So it came about, on the day of battle, that there was neither sword nor spear found in the hand of any of the people who were with Saul and Jonathan. But they were found with Saul and Jonathan his son (1 Samuel 13:22).

Imagine that! An entire army with no weapons.

Only the king and his son had any really efficient armaments.

No power. No resources. No army. No decent weapons. No hope?

Perhaps the people should wait for another day to work for their deliverance. Perhaps they should wait for the day of advantage. Perhaps they should do nothing for now, waiting for a more opportune moment. After all, dominion *doesn't* happen overnight. Peace isn't won in a day.

But, no.

Perhaps God desires for his people to "walk by faith, not by sight' (2 Corinthians 5:7). "Perhaps ...," thought Jonathan, "it may be that the Lord will work for us. For nothing restrains the Lord from saving by many or by few" (1 Samuel 14:6).

So he set out, just he and his armor bearer, alone, to attack the Philistine garrison. To gain the promised "peace of the land."

> Then Jonathan said, "Very well, let us cross over to these men, and we will show ourselves to them. If they say thus to us, 'Wait until we come to you,' then we will stand still in our place and not go up to them. But if they say thus, 'Come up to us,' then we will go up. For the Lord has delivered them into our hand, and this shall be the sign to us." So both of them showed themselves

to the garrison of the Philistines. And the Philistines said, "Look, the Hebrews are coming out of the holes where they have hidden." Then the men of the garrison called to Jonathan and his armor bearer, and said, "Come up to us, and we will show you something." So Jonathan said to his armor bearer, "Come up after me, for the Lord has delivered them into the hand of Israel." And Jonathan climbed up on his hands and knees with his armorbearer after him; and they fell before Jonathan. And as he came after him, his armorbearer killed them. That first slaughter which Jonathan and his armorbearer made was about twenty men within about half an acre of land. And there was trembling in the camp, in the field, and among all the people. The garrison and the raiders also trembled; and the earth quaked, so that it was a very great trembling (1 Samuel 14:8–15).

The odds were against him. One man with his armor bearer, against the entire Philistine garrison! It was suicidal.

Maybe. It *looked* that way. But then, looks can be deceiving. Appearances *are* sometimes quite out of line with facts.

So, what were the facts?

Jonathan knew that the land belonged to God, not to the Philistines (Psalm 24:1). He knew that God had placed the land into the care of His chosen people, the Jews (Joshua 1:2). He knew that they had sure and secure promises that if they would obey God's Word and do God's work, they would be prosperous and successful (Joshua 1:8), that every place which the sole of their feet trod would be granted to them (Joshua 1:3), and that no man would be able to stand before them all the days of their lives (Joshua 1:5). He knew that if the people would only "dwell in the shelter of the Most High," in the "shadow of the Almighty" (Psalm 91:1), He would deliver them "from the snare of the fowler And from the perilous pestilence" (Psalm 91:3). He would cover them "with his feathers" (Psalm 91:4), and protect them from "the terror by night" and "the arrow that flies by day" (Psalm 91:5). And though a thousand fall at their left hand, ten thousand to the right, affliction would not approach them; they would only look and see "the reward of the wicked" (Psalm 91:7–8). They would be protected from the teeth of the devourer, encompassed with supernatural power (Psalm 91:10).

These were the facts.

Though it *looked* as if God's people were broken, scattered, defeated, and woe begotten, in truth they were *more* than conquerors (Romans 8:37). They were overcomers (1 John 5:4).

Philistine dominion was *fiction*. Israel cowering in fear was foolish *fantasy*. Pessimism about their ability to stand and not be shaken (Hebrews 12:28) was novel *nonsense*.

Jonathan knew that.

So, he acted. He acted boldly. He acted decisively. He acted on the basis of the *truth* and *reliability* of God's Word, not on the seemingly impossible circumstances that faced him. He acted on faith and not on sight. He acted *realistically*, knowing that God's definition of things is the *real* reality, the *only* reality. He acted with passion and zeal for the things he *knew* to be God's will.

And God honored him. He blessed Jonathan with great success. Unbelievable success.

Jonathan stood against the tide. By all rights, he should have been crushed under its weight, but instead, the tide turned! He won the day and saved the nation.

Faith and Victory

"Now faith is the substance of things hoped for, the evidence of things not seen" (Hebrews 11:1). "By it the elders obtained a good testimony" (Hebrews 11:2). Against all odds, against all hope they obtained victory. They snatched glory out of the jaws of despair. They hurdled insurmountable obstacles to "lay hold" of the good things of the Lord (Hebrews 6:18). By faith, they believed God for the remarkable, for the impossible (Matthew 19:26; Hebrews 11:1–40): Abraham (Genesis 12:1–4), Sarah (Genesis 18:11–14), Isaac (Genesis 27:27–29), Jacob (Genesis 48:1–20), Joseph (Genesis 50:24–26), Moses (Exodus 14:22– 29), Rahab (Joshua 6:23), Ruth (Ruth 1:16–17), Gideon (Judges 6:1–8:35), Barak (Judges 4:1–5:31), Samson ((Judges 13:1–16:31), Jephthah (Judges 11:1–12:7), David (1 Samuel 16:1–17:58), Isaiah (Isaiah 1:1–6:13), Samuel, and all the prophets 0 Samuel 1:1–28; Hebrews 11:32). For by faith they "subdued kingdoms, worked righteousness, obtained promises, stopped the mouths of lions, quenched the violence of fire, escaped the edge of the sword, out of weakness were made strong, became valiant in battle, turned to flight the armies of the aliens" (Hebrews 11:33–34). Though they were mocked and persecuted, imprisoned and tortured, impoverished and oppressed, they were unshaken and eventually obtained Gods great reward (Hebrews 11:35–40).

> Therefore we also, since we are surrounded by so great a cloud of witnesses, let us lay aside every weight, and the sin which so easily ensnares us, and let us run with endurance the race that is set before us, looking unto Jesus, the author and fin-

isher of our faith, who for the joy that was set before Him endured the cross, despising the shame, and has sat down at the right hand of the throne of God (Hebrews 12:1–2).

The future is ours.

But the days are urgent. Humanism's empire of perversity and idolatry, of greed and gluttony, is collapsing like a house of cards. Peace is nowhere to be found.

The battlefields of Eastern Europe, Southeast Asia, Central America, and the Middle East give vivid testimony that humanism's hope for peace on earth is a false hope. The economic ruin of Nicaragua, Ethiopia, Afghanistan, Poland, and Russia give vivid testimony that humanism's hope for utopia is a false hope. The ovens of Auschwitz, the abortuaries of L.A., the bathhouses of New York, and the nurseries of Bloomington give vivid testimony that humanism's hope of medical and genetic perfectibility is a false hope. The ghettos of Detroit, the barrios of West San Antonio, the tent cities of Phoenix, and the slums of St. Louis give vivid testimony that humanism's hope of winning the "war on poverty" is a false hope.

But the Biblical hope has *never* yet been found wanting.

So, what are we waiting for?

There is starving in the shadow of plenty. There is a job that must be done. And only we can do it.

Oh, sure, it is a monumental task. There is no denying that to tackle the hunger, homelessness, and hopelessness that blights our land will require massive resources, unending commitment, and diligent labor. Dominion doesn't happen overnight. Peace isn't won in a day.

But ... God has given us His blueprints. And His plan cannot fail.

It must be admitted that "there are giants in the land" (Numbers 13:33) and that "we appear to be grasshoppers in our own sight, and in theirs ..." (Numbers 13:33).

But ... God has given us His promises. And His Word cannot fail.

Certainly, long term unemployment, the deinstitutionalization of mental patients, old age dependencies, urban gentrification and displacement, rural land foreclosures, industrial layoffs, and massive illiteracy are complex problems that cannot be solved with wishful thinking or naive and simplistic executive action.

But ... God has established His priorities, laid out His strategies, and illumined His principles. And His program cannot fail.

Time to Go to Work

Jonathan faced the Philistines. He took God at His Word. He went to work, and emerged victorious. Against all odds, Ehud faced the power of Moab (Judges 3:12–30); Shaingar faced the power of the Philistines (Judges 3:31); Deborah faced the power of Canaan (Judges 4:1–5:31); Gideon faced the power of Midian (Judges 6:1–8:35); the apostles faced the power of the Roman empire (Acts 8:1–28:31); and each one emerged victorious.

Against all odds!

Isn't it about time for us to demonstrate to an unbelieving world that God can still beat the odds? Isn't it about time for us to prove to a fallen and depraved generation that God can raise up a weak and unesteemed people against all odds, and win? Isn't it about time we laid the foundation of peace? Isn't it?

> For though we walk in the flesh, we do not war according to the flesh. For the weapons of our warfare are not carnal but mighty in God for pulling down strongholds, casting down arguments and every high thing that exalts itself against the knowledge of God, bringing every thought into captivity to the obedience of Christ (2 Corinthians 10:3–5).

We are invincible (Ephesians 6:10–18; Romans 8:37–39). Even the gates of hell shall not prevail against us (Matthew 16:8). If, that is, we would only do our job. If we would only take the Gospel hope beyond, to "the ends of the earth" (Acts 1:8), if we would only "make disciples of all the nations" (Matthew 28:19), if we would only "rebuild the ancient ruins ... raise up the age old foundations ... and repair the breach" (Isaiah 58:12) by caring for the poor, the afflicted, and the dispossessed (Isaiah 58:10).

It is time to go to work. It is time to lay the foundations of peace. We may have to work with few, or even no resources. Jonathan did it. (1 Samuel 14:6). We may have to improvise, utilizing less than perfect conditions and less than qualified workers and less than adequate facilities. Nehemiah did it. (Nehemiah 1:20). We may have to battle the powers that be, the rulers and the principalities. Like Peter, James, and John (Acts 4:20). We may have to go with what we've got, with no support, no notoriety, and no cooperation. Like Jeremiah (Jeremiah 1: 4–10). We may have to start "in weakness, in fear, and in much trembling" (1 Corinthians 2:3), without "persuasive words of wisdom" (1 Corinthians 2:4). Like the Apostle Paul (1 Corinthians 2:1).

Instead of allowing their limitations and liabilities to discourage and debilitate them, the heroes of the faith went to work God's power being made manifest in their weakness (1 Corinthians 1:26–29).

It is time for *us* to go to work.

Dominion doesn't happen overnight. Peace isn't won in a day. So the sooner we get started, the better off we'll be. The sooner we get started, the quicker the victory will come. In order to get from here to there, we need to set out upon the road. At the very least.

There will never be an ideal time to *begin* the work of charity.

Money is *always* short. Volunteers are *always* at a premium. Facilities are always either too small, or too inflexible, or in the wrong location, or too expensive. There is *never* enough time, *never* enough energy, and *never* enough resources.

So what?

Our commission is not dependent upon conditions and restrictions. Our commission is dependent only upon the unconditional promises of God's Word. God has called us to peace (1 Corinthians 7:15), to be peacemakers (Matthew 5:9), "so then let us pursue the things that make for peace" (Romans 14:9).

We should just go. Do what we ought to. We should make peace. Starting *now*.

> There shall be no poor among you, since the Lord will surely bless you in the land which the Lord your God is giving you to possess as an inheritance, if only you carefully obey the voice of the Lord your God, to observe with care all these commandments which I command you today (Deuteronomy 15:4–5 NAS).

"There is no peace for the wicked." But if we will do our job, and do it now, then peace shall be reckoned unto us.

Conclusion

The tenth basic principle in the Biblical blueprint for welfare is that the work of charity is the foundation of peace and so must be undertaken now. The situation is urgent.

Jonathan knew the odds were against him, lopsidedly so, when he faced the Philistines single-handedly. But he also knew that God blessed obedience. He knew that God blessed valor. He knew that God's work done in God's way would never lack for God's provision and protection. So, he set out. And he won! He gained peace for the land.

We are called to "walk by faith, not by sight" (2 Corinthians 5:7). We are to walk in the supernatural anointing of Almighty God, casting down strongholds, taking every thought, every word, every deed, every man, woman and child captive for Christ.

We are not to tremble at the "giants in the land." For we have come as giant killers!

Ours is the "peace that surpasses all understanding." And it shall be a constant reality if we would only lay the foundation of peace, if we would only act charitably!

Summary

God desires for His people to obtain an inheritance of peace.

But unless we lay the foundation for peace, we shall never see that glorious day. And as Isaiah so clearly points out, that foundation is charity. *There will never be any peace until we do our job of caring for the poor.*

That of course will take time and energy. But we have to start somewhere. The story of Jonathan illustrates how important, how urgent, decisive action can be in times of great distress. Jonathan shows us how we can begin to turn things around, preparing for the day of peace.

It is time for us to go to work. It is time for us to evidence the kind of faith that challenges the stiffest odds. It is time for us to lay the foundation of peace. We must begin *now*, before it's too late.

PART II
THE BIBLICAL BLUEPRINT:
3 STRATEGIES

Only be strong and very courageous, that you may observe to do according to all the Law which Moses My servant commanded you; do not turn from it to the right hand or to the left, that you may prosper wherever you go. This Book of the Law shall not depart from your mouth, but you shall meditate in it day and night, that you may observe to do according to all that is written in it. For then you will make your way prosperous, and then you will have good success.

Joshua 1:7–8

11

WHAT THE GOVERNMENT SHOULD DO

In light of these ten basic principles in the Biblical blueprint for welfare, what should the government do?

Obviously, it shouldn't be doing what it is doing now.

In every way, shape, and form imaginable, government welfare obstructs compassion, short circuits efficiency, and stymies progress. Government welfare is a hopeless mess.

Wouldn't it be better to create a messless hope?

Only thirty cents of each antipoverty dollar actually reaches the poor. The other seventy cents is gobbled up by the government's lumbering bureaucracy. Thus, it takes lots and lots of dollars even to make a show of it. Not surprisingly, welfare spending in the U.S. has risen by at least 50% *every* year since the "war on poverty" was announced. Social welfare spending has *never* been cut—not in the Nixon administration, nor under Ford, Carter, Reagan, Bush, or Clinton.

What about the legacy of the Reagan administration? Despite all the liberal moaning and groaning and the media hype over so-called "budget cuts," the Reagan administration increased social welfare spending *every* year it held office. In 1981, it spent $68.7 billion more than the year before. In 1982, it spent $54.2 billion more than that. In 1983, it spent $45.8 billion more than that. And in 1984, it spent $39.6 billion more than that. The *only* thing it cut was the *rate* of increase in spending.

And what has this incomprehensible deluge of spending wrought? How are the lives of the poor improved?

They aren't. If anything, the poor are worse off than before the last six administrations spent billions of federal dollars.

Before the "war on poverty," 13% of Americans were poor, using the official definition, with an unemployment rate of 3.6%. After untold billions of dollars spent over the past two decades, 15% of Americans are now poor, using the official definition, with an unemployment rate that has ranged upwards as high as 11.6%, but never downward any lower than 4.2%. Obviously, we're losing ground.

The evidence for this astounding failure is irrefutable. Books like Walter Williams's *The State Against Blacks* (McGraw-Hill, 1982), Lawrence Mead's *Beyond Entitlement* (Free Press, 1986), Thomas Sowell's *The Economics and Politics of Race* (William Morrow, 1983), George Gilder's *Wealth and Poverty* (Basic Books, 1981), Clarence Carson's *The War on the Poor* (Arlington House, 1969), Charles Murray's *Losing Ground* (Basic Books, 1984), and Henry Hazlitt's *The Conquest of Poverty* (Arlington House, 1973), have shown beyond any shadow of a doubt that the welfare system is utterly unredeemable. But then, we don't really need experts and their mountains of statistics to tell us that.

Even attempts at reform—"in-kind" payments, workfare, negative income taxes, "right to work" laws, job retraining programs, and enterprise zoning—have miserably failed to shake loose the albatross of inefficiency and maladministration that hangs about the neck of government welfare.

Of course, the reason Christians must oppose welfare policies is not simply that they don't work. Christians must oppose government policies because they are *wrong*. They violate Scripture. That they don't work is icing on the cake!

So, what can be done?

Or better still, what *must* be done?

Paying People Not to Work

The whole idea behind Biblical charity is to get the poor back on their feet, working again, independent and productive. It seems that the whole idea behind government welfare is exactly the opposite. It knocks the poor off their feet, keeps them from working, creates long term dependencies, and makes them completely and entirely unproductive.

Government welfare *expects* next to nothing from its beneficiaries. It extends its privileges as unquestioned and unquestionable entitlements. The poor are not obligated in any way to meet the social demands of citizenship. In this way, welfare is an especially grotesque form of *discrimination*. It creates a *separate* class of people,

people who are not like all others in the society: They are not expected to act responsibly; they are not expected to learn a trade; they are not expected to support their families; they are not expected to improve their lot; they are not expected to stay out of trouble with the law. This absolute absence of expectation serves as an almost insurmountable *disincentive.*

Why should a ghetto teenager even try? Why not just take the path of least resistance? Why not just conform? Why not just *stay* in his *place?*

Talk about discrimination! Talk about oppressive racism!

Why should an unskilled, inexperienced teenager take menial jobs, slowly working his way up the ladder from poverty to productivity, when he could make a much better living for himself–initially–on welfare? In New York, welfare benefits available to the state's poor accrue to more than one-and-a-half times the minimum wage. Who in his right mind would go to work at McDonald's for $5.15 and hour when he could "earn" $6.75 an hour' on welfare? Only someone who is determined to get off the "new plantation," no matter what the cost. Today's "underground railroad" is a job. Unfortunately, the "railroad" rarely runs among the poorest of the poor.

Promiscuous handouts by the government inevitably shift the bottom third of the economy from the payrolls to the welfare rolls. In 1960, there were 3 million welfare recipients. Between 1968 and 1972, new cases were added at a double-digit increase rate, so that by the end of the Nixon administration, there were 10.8 million recipients. Today the numbers have gone into the astronomical range: Over 34.0 million Americans are on welfare as of 1998.

It only makes sense. Standing in lines, filling out forms, haunting the streets, and watching TV is, at first glance anyway, a whole lot more pleasant way to spend a week than digging ditches, pumping gas, or flipping hamburgers. Welfare is a trap. It is bondage.

The only way to remove work disincentives from the welfare system is to remove entitlements. If benefits are to be given at all, they should carry with them obligations, expectations, and responsibilities.

Entitlements are an oppressive bondage upon the poor. They are discriminatory. They are wicked.

> Is this not the fast that I have chosen: To loose the bonds of wickedness, To undo the heavy burdens, To let the oppressed go free, And that you break every yoke (Isaiah 58:6)?

Entitlements must go.

Minimum Wage Laws

Entitlements are not the only government sanctioned tools of discrimination. Minimum wage laws too, cause high unemployment among low-skilled workers, *eliminating* them from the mainstream of society.

Supposedly designed to protect workers on the lower end of the economy from exploitation, the laws actually work to exclude them from the economy altogether. After all, if a wage of $5.15 an hour *must* be paid to *every* worker, then what kind of workers will be hired? Very simply, *only* those whose skills are *"worth"* $5.15 an hour or more. If a laborer is inexperienced and unskilled, he has little chance of breaking into the market. The minimum wage then effectively *eliminates* the opportunities of the poor. Only crime is unencumbered by minimum wage laws. Ever wonder why street crime is so enticing to today's impoverished youth?

But, besides the questions of skill or experience, minimum wage laws also raise the question of *race*, to the detriment of minorities. If a racist employer is forced by the government to pay the same minimum wage to Blacks, Whites, and Hispanics, his hiring criterion ceases to be economic and becomes instead preferential. Whom will he hire, an unskilled, inexperienced black, or an unskilled, inexperienced white? By leveling the market interests, racists are *encouraged* to discriminate. Blacks and other minorities suffer.

When the first federal minimum wage law was passed back in 1953, the rate of black teenage unemployment and the rate of white teenage unemployment were the same: about 9%. Black teenage unemployment immediately went up, until today in some cities it is in the 50% range. But white teenage unemployment is still in the single-digit range.

Why? Are American employers more racist today than they were in 1953? That doesn't seem likely. But employers have to take a chance with "less desirable people." Hiring such people may produce resentment in the work force. It's easier to hire your foreman's nephew for the summer. Unless you can hire a "less desirable person" cheaper, of course. Then the nephew will have to shape up and meet the bid.

Teenage unemployment isn't a permanent condition. When teenagers get older, they get married. Married men are far better risks for employers. Married black males are mostly working people. They seldom suffer from double-digit unemployment levels. So the minimum wage law's effects are not permanent.

What the law does is to *delay the entry* of less motivated minority youths into the work force. These people lose early years of experience. They suffer extra years of rejection and frustration. Nobody tells them why employers refuse to hire them; they just know that nobody will hire them. So while their white peers and black middle-class peers are finishing high school and getting college degrees, they are standing around on street corners, getting angry.

The U.S. government spends billions each year on a program for young people called Head Start. The program gets ghetto children into the public schools earlier. Then, when they become teenagers, the minimum wage law takes over. Its effects are the very opposite of Head Start. We might call it the "Head Stop" program. Or maybe, "Head Down."

The legal right to make a bid is the foundation of economic freedom. "I'll do it for less!" is the number-one weapon for the economically disadvantaged. "I'll do it better!" is their second cry, their ladder out of misery.

Minimum wage laws make the first cry illegal. The second cry has to be proven on the job before it can be safely believed by an employer—and minimum wage laws make it illegal for the person to get the job.

Minimum wage laws pull up the ladder about the time the disadvantaged person first gets the idea that he has to work himself out of poverty. "Sorry, Charlie!"

Minimum wage laws are not just a minority or youth issue. Unions have traditionally supported the minimum wage laws. But again, their intentions, though seemingly honorable, have only restricted the job market, pricing the nonunion poor completely out of the economy. It has simply been a case of the haves excluding the have-nots. Minimum wage laws create protected zones for those workers who might otherwise face competition from people who are willing and able to bid their services for less than the minimum wage allows.

Minimum wage laws, and the unions and legislators that support them, have in effect, created a permanent welfare underclass, dependent on entitlements for their very existence. They have inflicted on the poor a yoke of bondage.

> Is this not the fast that I have chosen: To loose the bonds of wickedness, To undo the heavy burdens, To let the oppressed go free, And that you break every yoke (Isaiah 58:6)?

Minimum wage laws must go.

Occupational Licensing

Supposedly, it is in the "public interest" for government to regulate business and industry. Supposedly, without the restrictions placed by government on merchants, manufacturers, and service industries, the safety and security of the public would be at risk. Oppressors and exploiters and any other kind of unscrupulous profiteer would swoop into the economy, raping and pillaging the land. Supposedly.

That may or may not be, but one thing is certain: The regulation of businesses and occupations works to the detriment of the poor.

The poor have traditionally worked their way up out of poverty through peddling or trash hauling or taxiing or trucking or repairing or building. But now, due to the regulation of each of those occupations at the behest of organized labor and liberal legislators, the poor are excluded from the possibility of even entering into the market.

Peddlers, if allowed to exist at all, are required to buy expensive licenses, maintain careful records, and to restrict their activities to certain specified areas. Gone are the days of the roadside stands. Gone are the days of the hawkers in the streets. Gone even are the days of unrestricted garage sales and flea markets and craft fairs.

Trash hauling too has become a heavily regulated occupation. Load fees, safety requirements, and yearly licensing have all but made extinct the neighborhood trashman willing and able to haul away old refrigerators, yard rubbish, and cast off refuse. Replaced by professional corporations and unions, the poor have no opportunity to build their own businesses. Free enterprise is no longer free for them.

The taxicab industry is even worse. Because taxiing requires minimal skills and minimal capital outlay (all you need is a car), it has always attracted a large number of poor laborers. But no more. The taxi industry is so carefully regulated and restricted that, in New York City for example, the selling price for operators licenses runs as high as $100,000! To drive a taxi! The poor are *kept* in their *place*. They are *forced to* depend upon entitlements.

Trucking too once attracted the poor. It provided, for a minimum of overhead, an avenue for the poor to advance. Now though, due to regulation and restriction, the poor are priced out of the industry. Today an independent trucker is forced to have a capital outlay of between $100,000 and $500,000, just to get started!

Like the peddler, the trashman, the independent taxi driver, and the independent trucker, the neighborhood handyman is a fading memory of a once flourishing economy. The electrical and plumbing and small appliance repair trades are all so carefully regulated and restricted that it is no longer possible for a kid who is "good with his hands" to expect any kind of future as a handyman. What with licensing fees, trade restrictions, union limits, experience requirements, and decreed standardizations, the poor are never given the opportunity to compete.

Similarly, independent remodelers and carpenters have been squeezed out of the market by government regulations. Again, the old bugaboo, licensing, has proven to be the absolute ruin of many a craftsman. Unable to withstand the ever escalating costs of doing business with bureaucracy, the poor simply leave the trade.

In essence, government regulations and occupational licensing are nothing short of *economic sanctions* against the poor and disadvantaged. They force them to rely on the handouts of the welfare state. They are a yoke and are inconsistent with a truly free society.

Is this not the fast that I have chosen: To loose the bonds of wickedness, To undo the heavy burdens, To let the oppressed go free, And that you break every yoke (Isaiah 58:6)?

Occupational licensing must go.

Subsidized Industry

Union leaders and legislators claim that American industry must be subsidized in order to save the jobs of millions of American workers. They claim that basic heavy industries like steel, automobiles, textiles, rubber, and oil must be subsidized in order to survive.

Actually, quite the opposite is true.

Because American industry *has* been subsidized, the U.S. share of world trade declined 16% during the decade of the 60s, and another 23% during the decade of the 70s. And as a result, a, tremendous number of workers have lost their jobs. Between 1975 and 1990, nearly 22% of all manufacturing jobs in the U.S. ceased to exist. According to the Bureau of Labor statistics, another 30% will disappear between 1985 and the turn of the century.

So what has this dismal state of affairs to do with government subsidies?

Everything!

Because of the subsidies, industry has not been forced to deal with market trends. It has not had to modernize. It has not had to retool.

Declining industries have been artificially sustained. So, plant closures have been kept to a minimum, and bankruptcies have been staved off. But at what cost? Inefficient and antiquated factories, unhindered by market forces, end up squandering millions upon millions of dollars that could have been invested in *new* ventures opening up *more* job opportunities and *more* job security for the future.

The import controls, tax breaks, and regulatory relief measures that government and industry leaders have won for American companies have only intensified the high technology and high efficiency strategies of companies in Japan, South Korea, Brazil, and Germany. And that only pushes their American competitors further and further behind in the race for excellence and prosperity in the decades ahead.

It seems the more government meddles with the apparatus of the economy, the worse things get. Especially for the poor.

Give It Back to the Indians

The welfare state idea is a very old, old idea. The Incas subscribed to it. So did the Romans. But the model for our present system is actually a home grown heresy. When the 60s "war on poverty" activists were looking for something to replace the old Elizabethan Poor Law ethic, they had to look no further than the Washington office of the Bureau of Indian Affairs (BIA; a. k. a. the Office of Indian Affairs).

The Office of Indian Affairs (OIA) was established in 1824. It was operated by the War Department. In 1849, it was transferred to the newly created Bureau of the Interior. It is doubtful that any U.S. bureaucracy in the 19th century was more infamous, more riddled with corruption, than the Office of Indian Affairs.

The OIA ran the reservations. It created a *welfare state* for conquered tribes. It was understood as an instrument of *conquest* and *subjection*. The Indians were placed on the reservations in order to control them. There was no doubt about this in anyone's mind * The government funneled money down the bureaucracy, and the Indians wound up in poverty.

That's where they still are. There is no group beneath them. Every American realizes that the Indians are on the bottom of the pile: little hope, not much future, and not much money.

What most Americans don't understand is that the government funnels about a billion and a half dollars through the BIA every year. Now, there are about 735,000 Indians in the U.S. This means that the government spends $2,000 per year on every Indian—man, woman, and child. If families average six people, this is $12,000 a year.

Indians on the reservations pay no taxes, state, local, or federal. Thus, a reservation family can earn money without suffering any tax consequences. Furthermore, almost no zoning or other state and local regulations apply, so they can start any sort of business on the reservations.

Here we see the incredible failure of a socialist experiment that is well over a century old. The Indians are in poverty, yet the government is providing the BIA with enough money to make every Indian family middle class, and upper middle class if they earn as little as $5,000 per family.

Conclusion: the Indians aren't getting the money. The BIA bureaucracy is.

But this is only part of the story. The federal government owns the reservations' 52 million acres of land. It holds this land "in trust" for the Indians. Tribal councils (socialist bureaucracies) have some say in the use of the land. But only *some*.

R. J. Rushdoony served for a decade as a missionary to the Western Shoshone Indians in the Idaho-Nevada area. Here was his evaluation of the program in 1954:

> Whatever the pre-reservation Indian was—and his faults were real—he was able to take care of himself and had a character becoming to his culture and religion. He was a responsible person. Today he is far from that. The wretched security he has had, beginning with the food and clothing dole of early years, designed to enforce the reservation system and destroy Indian resistance, has sapped him of character. The average Indian knows that he can gamble and drink away his earnings and still be sure that his house and land will remain his own; and, with his hunting rights, he can always eke out some kind of existence.

> Government men too often hamper and impede the man with initiative and character. This is because their program inevitably must be formulated in terms of the lowest common denominator, the weakest Indian. In addition, the provisions of the government for the "welfare" and "security" of the Indians

remove the consequences from their sinning and irresponsibility. The result is a license to irresponsibility, which all the touted government projects cannot counteract." (R. J. Rushdoony, "Life on the Reservation," in *Essays on Liberty, Vol. 2* [Irvington-on-Hudson, New York: Foundation for Economic Education, 1954], pp. 49-50.)

So, having seen the system in action, the politicians voted for a national program for *all* the minority groups in the 60s. The results were predictable to anyone who had ever been on a reservation. The promises by the politicians were the same sorts of promises given to the Indians. "Just do what we say, Chief, and you'll be taken care of."

It isn't the Indians who are the Indian-givers; it's the welfare state politicians.

Why not create profit-seeking corporations for every tribe, turn all the BIA property (including the land) over to these corporations, and distribute the shares on a per capita basis to every family head?

Why not allow these corporations to operate federal tax-free for, say, ten years?

Why not allow the reservations to retain their "zero tax, zero regulations" status? They could become "free trade zones" overnight. Businesses would flock to them.

In short, why not take the whole reservation system and give it back to the Indians?

Why not? Because it would cripple the bureaucracy, that's why not! It would set dangerous precedents for all of the other "kept" minorities, that's why not! It would eliminate the entire welfare mentality, that's why not!

A Policy for the New Millennium

So what should the government do? How can the humanitarians and philanthropists who create public policy actually render aid to the needy in our land?

Very simply, government should *return* to the free enterprise system. The government should take every measure to ensure that ours is once again a "Land of Opportunity."

Welfare entitlement programs should be completely dismantled and eliminated.

Minimum wage laws should be abolished.

Occupational licensing restrictions should be kept to a bare minimum—for the purposes of public safety only.

Industry subsidies and protectionist trade policies should never even be considered.

In short, the government should get out of the way!

If legislators and union leaders would only realize that by reducing the level of interference in the economy and by ridding the nation of various constraints on the market, they could help the poor more than welfare, food stamps, and Social Security ever have, maybe a real "war on poverty" could be fought in this land of plenty. Jobs would be created, work incentives would abound, investment would be stimulated, productivity would soar, and technology would advance. And the poor would benefit from a turn around like that, *more* than anyone else.

But legislators and union leaders refuse to make that kind of turn around. Thus it is not at all unreasonable to ask, "Do union leaders *really* want to help the poor? Do "liberal" politicians *really* care? Or is all their talk of "fairness" and "justice" just rhetoric to manipulate the masses? The truth about minimum wage laws was widely exposed over twenty years ago. Concerned, thinking people have argued for its abolition for two decades. They are still here.

Sinful men dominate our society, men who really *don't* care about the poor at all. We can expect no help from them.

In the Meantime

Ultimately the sinful men who dominate our society, those who have encumbered the poor with the bondage of welfarism, must be ousted from their places of influence and power. We must *vote them out.* But, that may take quite a while.

So, what do we do in the meantime? And how do we prepare for the transition?

First, the church must take up her philanthropic mantle *now,* even before the welfare state has been dismantled. No real political action can be taken to transfer welfare responsibilities to the church if the church is unprepared, inexperienced, and uninspired. Conservatives have been rabble-rousing for years about how churches and families can do a better job of taking care of the poor than the government. It's time to *prove it.* No one in Washington is going to take significant steps toward eliminating public welfare programs if we don't start developing *real and reliable alternatives.* If welfare were abolished tomorrow, millions of Americans would suffer calamitously. The short-term chaos would virtually offset any long-term benefits. The church isn't ready to take up her responsibilities, so she needs to *get ready.* Only then can we expect tangible political reform.

Second, we must begin a program of privatization similar to the Thatcher initiatives that were launched several years ago in Great Britain by Margaret Thatcher. For more than eight years the ruling Conservative Party in England slowly, quietly, and efficiently returned billions of dollars of government property and resources to the private sector. Socialized welfare programs were gradually but systematically surrendered into the hands of the citizenry. The entire economy was moved toward the healthy decentralized free market system that made Britain great in the first place. Similar measures in the U. S. could see the gradual transfer of public and subsidized housing to the tenants. They would become *homeowners* instead of federal dependents. Don't you know that the quality of those projects would instantly improve? Privatization could arrange for the transfer of federal properties to various functioning charities. It could also provide for the transfer of responsibility from the well-heeled but ineffective government bureaucracies to the cash-poor but efficiently run private sector. Washington would save billions, the charities would gain essential properties and resources, and the poor would be compassionately cared for in a way never before possible.

Third, a number of economic steps could be taken to encourage the re-mantling of private welfare and the dis-mantling of public welfare. Tax credits—or better yet dollar for dollar tax reductions—could be implemented for all donations to legitimately functioning local relief charities. This would encourage a much needed infusion of capital into the private sector. But it would also send a much needed message to Washington: People would rather pay Peter and Paul than they would Caesar Augustus, especially when what they're paying for is kindness and compassion. Since this kind of measure would only be temporary—until the public-to-private transfer was completed—questions of legitimacy could be handled by temporary certification boards appointed locally by participating churches and private agencies.

Fourth, enterprise zones should be established in the inner cities. Where urban renewal failed, free enterprise can succeed magnificently if only given the chance. Look what it has done for that tiny resourceless rock on the tip of China: Hong Kong. There is no other way to explain its fabulous productivity and unlimited opportunity. *Free* enterprise, ethically restrained by God's standards can transform poverty into productivity like nothing else on earth. It could turn our slums into hives of industry and centers of entrepreneurial zeal. But we must *free* businesses and property owners in those areas of governmental interference, overbearing taxation, and trade restrictions.

Once these measures have been enacted, only then can the "reservation" system of the welfare state be abolished. Only then will the elimination of entitlements, minimum wage laws, occupational licensing, and industrial subsidies be even remotely feasible in the political arena.

Of course, in order for these measures to even be considered, significant changes will have to occur in the lives and the thinking of America's citizens. Revival will have to erupt. Political reformation cannot precede spiritual reformation. Government cannot get *out* of the way if the church does not get *in* the way.

Thus, we must turn to the church.

Conclusion

In order for us to fully implement the Biblical blueprint for charity we must get the government *out* of the way. Government welfare is inefficient, unproductive, and destructive.

Entitlement programs discriminate against the poor by keeping them out of the work force.

Similarly, minimum wage laws, occupational licensing, subsidized industries, and protectionist trade policies, though designed to protect the populace and save jobs, actually only deepen the downward spiral of unemployment and privation. They become a trap, a yoke for the poor.

Thus, government must move away from its recent pattern of interventionism and restriction and toward a genuinely free market. Government must create opportunity by leaving the economy alone.

It is time government took some real affirmative action by providing equal opportunity to all men, including the poor, the unskilled, and the inexperienced.

Summary

Government welfare, because it is *completely out of line* with God's plan and purpose, inevitably does *more harm than good.*

Entitlements, minimum wage laws, occupational licensing, and industrial subsidies all work to undermine the opportunities of the poor. They are in effect *economic sanctions* against the poor.

Unfortunately, because the private sector and the church have been so complacent for so long, an immediate dismantling of the welfare system would cause short term chaos. Therefore we need to begin immediately implementing steps of transition: church programs, privatization, tax credits, enterprise zones, and deregulation.

Once these steps of transition have been adequately undertaken we can then get the government *completely* out of the welfare business.

12

WHAT THE CHURCH SHOULD DO

In the mid-nineteenth century, the prominent English economist John Stuart Mill pointed out that the difficulty of leaving relief entirely to private charity is that such charity operates "uncertainly and casually ... (it) lavishes its bounty in one place, and leaves people to starve in another."

His charge has yet to be adequately answered. That must change.

If conservative Christians are going to oppose the federal dole, then they must come up with workable alternatives. They must realize that it is foolish and fruitless to try and fight something with nothing.

We need alternatives. We need models.

Application must be undertaken. It is not enough to know that the socialistic and humanistic experiments in the "war on poverty" have been dismal failures. It is not enough to know that the "social Gospel" approach to ministry proposed by liberal Christians is in adequate and impotent. It is not even enough to formulate dynamic theological affirmations from our academic ivory towers. We must get our hands dirty in the work of caring for the poor, correctly, sanely, and Biblically. We must translate the basic principles of Biblical charity into basic strategies for Biblical charity.

Despite the magnitude of the Biblical evidence to the contrary, the church has, over the last generation, acted as if charity was not particularly important. We have allowed the powers and principalities, the governments and bureaucracies to steal away from us this particular duty, simply because we haven't seen it as central to the Gospel mission.

What has been the result of this neglect? A loss of the church's authority. Remember the fundamental Biblical principle of dominion: *dominion through service*. Authority flows to those individuals and institutions that voluntarily take responsibility.

As in the education of our children, in the administration of our hospitals, and in the dissemination of our culture, the church has lost control of the apparatus of charity in our society because the church has been in a conscious and deliberate *retreat* from the world. We've become so heavenly minded that we're no earthly good!

Our Perilous Times

Ours are perilous times. Virtually all the experts agree. Western civilization seems bent on a collision course with disaster.

Military strategists tell us that with more countries joining the nuclear arms race and worldwide terrorism on the rise, "Wars and rumors of wars" will soon be nostalgically recalled as "the joyous days of old."

Environmentalists tell us that due to gross negligence and mismanagement, the ecological balance of planet Earth is in very real jeopardy. In fact, they say, vast regions of our globe are now little more than semi-civilized hazardous waste dumps.

Economists tell us that the Third World is irrevocably buried beneath an avalanche of need, while the super powers are frozen in unproductive patterns of sloth and envy. The shift from the assembly lines to the breadlines will continue to be one of the most prominent features of the economic landscape in many countries.

On and on and on they go. Doom-sayers at every turn. Meteorologists say that, because of shifts in the global weather patterns, we can expect one natural catastrophe after another. Agricultural experts are predicting dire days of shortages and even famines just ahead. Sociologists, fearing a massive collapse of confidence and cultural apathy, can talk of little else.

And, as if all that were not enough, it appears as if a moral degeneration has set in as well. "Eat, drink, and be merry, for tomorrow we may die" has become the ethical emblem of an entire generation. Standards are crumbling. Morality is vanishing. Same sex marriages are becoming as common as sexual scandals among various high-profile public officials. Faithfulness and other such Victorian notions have been washed away by a tidal wave of promiscuity, vice, and corruption. Drugs, pornography, lawlessness, homosexuality, terrorism, abortion, rape, and infanticide have actually become commonplace. It seems as if nothing is sacred any longer.

So, what do these experts recommend? What hope can they offer us?

Some play the part of Machiavelli, advocating a central and all-powerful state. Deferment of a few individual liberties is a small price to pay for corporate survival, they say.

Some play the part of Peter Pan, saying, in effect, "Que sera, sera. Whatever will be, will be." "Let the cards fall where they may," they tell us, "There is no need to get all worked up about things we can't do anything about. Live and let live. Grab for all the gusto and forget about the mess we're in."

Others simply shrug their shoulders and, like Gaughin, effect a "Whence? What? and Whither?" despondency.

But regardless of their ideology and predisposition to action or inaction, the experts, with one voice, assert that stability in the Western world is indeed on a short tether. Change is in the wind.

Sowing and Reaping

How has this come to be? How could we, who had risen to such heights, have plunged to such depths?

The Bible teaches that there is a direct cause and effect principle at work in our culture, and in fact, in all cultures. There always has been and there always will be.

When a civilization takes seriously the commands of God for every area of life, it will be blessed. When its laws are in conformity with the Scriptural standards, when its institutions emulate the Scriptural models, when its character is shaped by the Scriptural edicts, then it will prosper and flourish (Deuteronomy 28:–14).

If, on the other hand, a civilization ignores the commands of God for every area of life, it will be cursed. When its laws are in disharmony with Scriptural standards, when its institutions contradict the Scriptural models, when its character defies the Scriptural edicts, it will flounder and fail (Deuteronomy 28:15–68).

Christianity was once the authoritative voice and conscience of Western culture. Erected upon a Biblical base, the culture flowered magnificently. In every realm, from the arts to the sciences, incredible advances were made. Blessing was evidenced round about in abundance.

But in recent years our culture has witnessed a coup d'état, a bloodless revolution. Christianity has been overthrown and replaced by a totally contrary world and life view called humanism. This is the primary cause of our cultural decline. The principle faith of our people has slowly eroded from Biblical productivity to humanistic irresponsibility.

Humanism is, according to Dr. Francis A. Schaeffer, "The placing of man at the center of all things and making him the measure of all things." Or, as Aleksandr Solzhenitsyn has said, it is "the proclaimed and practiced autonomy of man from any higher force above him." According to humanism, there is no notion of absolute right and wrong. There are no clear-cut standards: Standards flex with the whims of fashion. According to humanism, men's passions are not to be restrained. Passions are to be unshackled, floating free in the ever-shifting, ever-changing currents of the day. Humanism tosses to the wind that which made the blessings of Western culture possible: obedience to the unchanging, inerrant Law of God.

Taken together, the lessons of history and the lessons of Scripture are clear enough. If we sow seeds of obedience to God's Law, we will reap a bounteous harvest of blessing. If we sow seeds of rebellion against God's Law, we will reap a destitute harvest of cursing (Galatians 6:7). If we sow Christian principles, our culture will reap productivity, stability, and justice. If we sow humanistic principles, our culture will reap perversity, unrest, and tyranny.

Statisticians may pour over their flow charts from now until the end of time, but they will never discover another viable explanation for the rise and fall of cultures. None other exists.

So, back to our original question: How is it that we have come so close to the brink of destruction? Very simply, we have yielded to a humanistic world and life view, a view that contravenes the Word of God at every turn.

When we violate God's Law of gravity, we suffer very clear and obvious consequences. Is it any wonder that when we violate God's Laws of economics, or civics, or psychology, or philosophy, or science, or morality, we should similarly suffer clear and obvious consequences? Not hardly.

Humanism is wreaking havoc in catastrophic proportions simply because it is out of step with reality. Only God's Laws fit what is there. Thus, only God's Laws can lay foundations for peace, prosperity and genuine social security.

Humanism, and the culture which it spawns, are but dust in the wind.

The Failure of the Church

So Christianity has been overthrown as the foundational authority in Western culture. No longer is the Bible the final court of appeal in matters of law, economics, or ethics. Thus, the very nature of Western culture is undergoing a dramatic metamorphosis. It is undergoing a comprehensive philosophical and moral reversal. This radical reversal is not occurring because our civilization has been overrun by bands of barbarians from the hinterlands. It is not occurring because the Communists have been successful in infiltrating and sabotaging our governmental apparatus. It is not occurring because Madison Avenue has corrupted our youth. It is occurring because of the ineptness of the church. It is occurring because we Christians have failed.

Despite multimillion dollar budgets, despite a gargantuan constituency, despite a millennium-long legacy, the church has failed. Why? Why, on the very doorstep of the largest, most powerful, richest, best organized, and most vocal evangelical Christian movement ever, is this immoral, unstable, and humanistic mentality able to control the cultural apparatus? By all rights, evil ought to be converted and contained by the church, but the very opposite is true. Why? Why have Christians been so ineffective and unproductive in the world?

Why? Because Christians have abandoned the world. We have abandoned our God-ordained commission to be salt and light (Matthew 5:13–16). We have abandoned our dominion mandate (Genesis 1:28). Instead, we have emphasized a view of spirituality that is based on the pagan teachings of Plato. Accordingly, a sharp division is generally made between the "spiritual" and the "material." Since the "spiritual" realm is considered superior to the "material," all things physical, all things temporal, and all things earthly are spurned. Art, music, and ideas are ignored except for their value as propaganda. Activities that do not significantly contribute to piety are neglected. The Christian intellect is held suspect, if not altogether shunned. And pleasures of the flesh, regardless of how innocent or sacred, are condemned outright.

According to this popular perspective, all our efforts should be directed toward producing individualistic piety. Bible study, prayer, church attendance, and evangelism compose the totality of tasks for the Christian. Anything and everything else is a distraction and is worldly. Certainly, with this fortress mentality, we would never condone confronting the prevailing assumptions of the fallen culture nor constructing a program of reform for society.

As righteous as all this may sound at first hearing, it is patently unscriptural. Although the Biblical mandate includes as an integral aspect of its plan for victory deep devotion, piety, and holiness (Matthew 5:48), it also requires us to think hard about the nature of Christian civilization (1 Peter 1:13), to try to develop Biblical alternatives to humanistic civilization (Matthew 18:15–20), and to prophesy Biblically to the cultural problems of our age (Isaiah 6:8). These things, too, are true piety.

According to the Bible, "The earth is the Lord's, and all its fullness" (Psalm 24:1). But, in the minds of many believers, only the spirit is the Lord's. All else is tainted beyond reclamation by the stench of sin. According to the Bible, Jesus is Lord over the totality of life (Colossians 1:15–17; Hebrews 1:2–3). But, in the minds of many believers, Jesus is Lord, but only over a "religious cubbyhole" in life. According to the Bible, Christians are to confront, transform, and lead human culture (Matthew 5:13–16). But in the minds of many believers, Christians are to withdraw from human culture in order to focus on "religious" exercises.

By clinging to a defective, incomplete view of Christ's Lordship, we scuttle ourselves into a cultural backwater. By clinging to a defective, incomplete view of spirituality, we imprison ourselves within an evangelical ghetto. By clinging to a defective, incomplete view of spirituality, we minimize all impact, we sequester all significance, and we stifle all hope.

Rather than nurturing the flock of God and the world at large with the rich truths of practical Biblical instruction, we indulge in theological junk food. Rather than building all of life upon the unwavering foundation of God's Word, we humor ourselves with intellectual white elephants.

Is it any wonder that the sober secularists have captured the attentions of our leaders? Is it any wonder that the humanists have moved with ease into the vacuum? Is it any wonder that Christianity has been overthrown as the foundational authority in Western culture? The Bible has answers to the great and perplexing problems of our perilous times, but because the church has failed, those answers have gone largely unheard.

The collapse of Western culture, thus, has two "culprits." First, there is inhuman humanism; but there also is irrelevant, passive Christianity.

Standing at the Crossroads

Our culture, thus, stands at the crossroads. On the brink of crisis due to the twin evils of an aggressive, godless humanism and a passive, irrelevant church, we now must make a choice. We can either do nothing while our loved ones march glibly down the road to ruin, or we can reclaim all areas of life and culture to the sanity of Scriptural moorings. The choice is ours.

... Choose for yourselves this day whom you will serve.... But as for me and my house, we will serve the Lord (Joshua 24:15).

Okay. So, *what* do we do? What *should* the church do? Now that we're at the crossroads, which way should we go?

First, we must *stop* our incessant retreat. We must advance. We must begin to rebuild the ruins and repair the breach and restore the foundation (Isaiah 58:12). And, as ought to be quite evident by now, the way *that* is done is to care for the poor. Pseudo-piety is reversed and humanism is put on the defensive when we give ourselves to the hungry and satisfy the desire of the afflicted (Isaiah 58:10–11). All of culture must be reclaimed for Christ: politics, art, music, science, medicine, law, architecture, economics, agriculture, and literature, but the place to *begin* is charity.

Second, we must stop *talking* about it, *theorizing* about it, and *formulating* our strategies for it, and just *do* it. We must become Good Samaritans, not just ideologically or theologically, but *practically.* (My book, *Bringing in the Sheaves: Transforming Poverty into Productivity,* [currently in its third revised edition and available from Standfast Books, P.O. Box 1601, Franklin, TN 37065] provides a step-by-step plan for establishing a poverty ministry in the local church.) We must go to work and leave the excuses behind.

Returning to the Word

But where do we start? How do we actually set our hand to the task?

The whole reason the church abandoned the world in the first place was that Platonic theologies so corrupted our vision that we actually abandoned the Word. Thus, we must *return* to the Word. Doing our job depends on this.

The Bible is the *Word* revealed. Though we have professed belief in the Bible, we perpetuate a drought of Scriptural instruction within the local church and the spectacularization of half-truths. It is amazing to witness the fascinations many Christians entertain today. Demonology, angelology, and eschatology have each been bloated beyond recognition by unverifiable horror stories of hitch-hiking angels, trilateral conspiracies, "beast-coded" social security checks, and backward masking in rock music. To be certain, we are living in a day of unmitigated evil. Our culture is velvet-lined with corruption. There is little doubt in the minds of God's people that we are seeing accelerated occultic activity, abandonment of traditional values, and domination by systematic injustice. But our imbalance, imprecision, and inconsistency have deterred us from our tasks. We are called to be Christ's ambassadors, not investigative reporters. We are ministers of a new covenant, not marshals for a witch hunt. Until our preaching and teaching reflect a Biblical agenda, we will continue to be harassed by the tangential ravings of the fantastic. Rumor will prevail. Surely we can call sin "sin," stand by our convictions, and sound the prophetic alarms without indulging in nonsense (Proverbs 6:16–19; Amos 8:11–12).

We have *abandoned* the Word. This hermeneutical irresponsibility in turn encourages moral irresponsibility.

Christ is the *Word* incarnate. And our moral laxity, our ethical irresponsibility, has led us to abandon Him. We have left our first love (Revelation 2:4). Our addiction to mediocre scholarship and preaching has proven itself a spawning ground for a "devil-made-me-do-it" generation. And our escapist worship has created an escapist faith. As long as we can lay off on someone or something else the responsibility for sin, we feel we can escape its consequences. This wholesale denial of basic Biblical principles has short-circuited the very effectiveness and productivity of our ministries, but worse, it has set us at enmity with our Lord, the Captain of Life, Christ Himself.

Scripture lays upon believers the awesome task of introducing help, hope, and healing in a hurting land. When a culture fails morally, Scripture looks to the impotent witness of the church as first cause (2 Chronicles 7:14). Judgement befalls a people when the saints refuse to humble themselves. Sickness in a society is not measured by conspiracies, manifestations, or political orientation, but by the dearth of costly discipleship among God's own (Galatians 6:7; James 1:14–15).

We have abandoned the Word. Hermeneutical irresponsibility and moral irresponsibility lead inevitably to ecclesiastical irresponsibility.

Communion is the *Word* made manifest. But our spiritually polluted thinking has reduced Sacramental worship to a mere ceremonial nicety. We dispatch our task of making present among the people an awareness of the reality of the New Covenant (1 Corinthians 11:25), of the Body of Christ (1 Corinthians 11:24), and of the divine sacrifice on Calvary (1 Corinthians 11:26). Instead, we embrace a breezy, empty-headed extemporaneity, short on content, but long on "feel-good" experience. In the garden, Eve committed adultery with the serpent by eating his *food*, thus *wedding* herself to the corruption of the world (2 Corinthians 11:2–3; Genesis 3:1–13). Communion is the marriage *supper* of the Lamb wherein our unity with Christ is "remembered" and made manifest. To abandon it is to go the way of Eve, the way of Cain, to rush headlong into the error of Balaam, and ultimately to perish in the rebellion of Korah (Jude 11).

Hermeneutical irresponsibility. Moral irresponsibility. Ecclesiastical irresponsibility.

All because "we have *abandoned* the Word: the Word revealed, the Word incarnate, and the Word made manifest in the Lord's Supper.

If there is to be any agenda for the church in the days ahead, this is it: Return to the Word.

What has this to do with poverty relief?

Everything. Absolutely everything.

Any kind of group or organization can operate a soup kitchen, open a shelter, give away cheese and butter, redistribute wealth, and provide a job service. But only the church can provide the things that the poor need the most. Only the church—as she holds steadfastly to the Word revealed, the Word incarnate, and the Word made manifest—can transform poverty into productivity.

This is due to several great truths.

First, the church *renews the minds* of the poor through the teaching of the Word. Right doctrine shatters old habits, explodes bad thoughts, and establishes *real* hope. The Gospel *changes* people. Thus, our charity agenda must not simply be one more conservative, deregulated, family-centered, work-oriented, and decentralized program. It must be forthrightly evangelistic. The poor need good news. They need *the* Good News.

Second, the church readjusts the poor to both God's society and the world in worship, through the Lord's Supper. To take the Lord's Supper is not to indulge in an abstract theological ritual. It is a tangible offering *to* God, a consecration *before* God, a communion *with* God, and a transformation *in* God. It is thus a conscious drive at the heart of reality. In this simple yet profound act of worship, the meaning and value of all life is revealed and fulfilled. The poor, like all men, need a double dose of reality. And only the church can serve up that reality as she gathers around the sacramental altar.

Third, the church reforms the life styles of the poor. The discipling and disciplining process of life in the local church repatterns a man's ways according to the ways of the Lord.

As we bring up our children "in the nurture and admonition of the Lord" (Ephesians 6:4 KJV), there are several measures that we must diligently undertake to ensure that "when they are old, they will not depart" from "the way they should go" (Proverbs 22:6). So, for instance, we redirect their childish foolishness (Proverbs 22:15) by instilling in them Godly *habits*. Through *ritual* and *repetition* we *train* them to walk the "paths of justice" (Proverbs 2:8) and to avoid the "ways of darkness" (Proverbs 2:13). Through routines of righteousness we *establish* them in "every good path" (Proverbs 2:9) so that they may ever afterward "trust in the Lord with all (their) heart, And lean not on (their) own understanding, In all (their) ways acknowledging Him," so that then "He shall direct (their) paths" (Proverbs 3:5–6).

But not only do we seek to build in the lives of our children Godly habits, we are concerned to immerse them in the life of the community of faith. Knowing that "bad company corrupts good character" (1 Corinthians 15:33 NIV), we strive to surround our children with good influences, with righteous role models, with positive reinforcement, and with joyous fellowship.

And finally, as we raise our children we provide constructive chastisement. When they violate God's standards, we discipline them (Proverbs 13:24). This "boundary of fear" restrains them from ill, and protects them from evil (Proverbs 1:8–9; Proverbs 23:13–14).

What does this have to do with a church's ministry to the poor? Quite a bit, as it turns out. You see, like our children, the poor desperately need life style adjustments that only life in the Body can effect. The *ritual of* worship and consistent discipleship trains them in humility, joy, perseverance, diligence, and responsibility, and gives them a "new song." It instills in them Godly habits. It *repatterns* them according to the ways of God.

Through constant fellowship within the community of faith, the poor have these new habits reinforced. Their expectations and desires are slowly brought into conformity with the expectations and desires of the righteous. They are *reformed*.

And finally, the "boundary of fear" restrains the poor from old patterns of sloth and self-destruction. Through work requirements, moral expectations, and community obligations, all enforced by church discipline (Matthew 18:15–20; 1 Corinthians 5:1–13), they are encouraged to grow in grace and maturity. They learn that their attitudes, actions, and inactions have very real consequences (Galatians 6:7). They who are "weary and heavy laden" are *liberated* from the slave market shackles of the world and are yoked with the "gentle" and "easy" discipline of Christ instead (Matthew 11:28–30).

An Agenda for the Future

For the church, the agenda is plain and simple: Return to the Word that renews the minds of the poor; return to the Word that readjusts them to God's society and the world; return to the Word that reforms their life styles.

According to the Word, the church is the protector of covenant families. Thus, after Gospel and Sacrament, the first item on the church's agenda is to get those families in order. The deacons should systematically visit every family in the church, teaching them providence, thrift, and planning. They should teach the discipline of budgeting, the routine of Godly stewardship, and the necessity to provide adequately for dependents. So, for instance, the deacons should see to it that every wife is covered by a low-cost term insurance policy on her husband's life. They should also make sure that each family has a good, reliable health plan. To place the church's membership under the fearful threat of having the moral obligation to support a destitute family is wrong when low-cost insurance is available to offset the risk. If necessary, the deacons can use church funds to pay the premiums until the family's breadwinner can get control over his finances.

Second, the church should set up a charity outreach program with food pantries, sheltering options, emergency counseling, referral resources, clothes closets, etc. (Again, for a comprehensive plan of implementation, see my book, *Bringing in the Sheaves* from Standfast Books.)

Third, successful churches should help poor churches set up similar indigenous care programs. They can also do such things as provide scholarship money for poor families' children to attend Christian schools. Or better yet, churches with schools can teach pastors in poor churches how to set up and run a local Christian school. This is vital if Christians are ever to break the domination of the humanist state.

Deacons in churches that have developed successful family financial budgeting programs can work, with deacons in poorer churches to set up similar programs. (Programs such as *Financial Peace* available from Dave Ramsey at **FinancialPeace.com** and *Christian Financial Concepts* from Larry Burkett at **CFCMinistry.org** have all sorts of helpful books, workbooks, and software packages. Each family should be instructed to do monthly—or at least quarterly—budgeting by using one of these programs. Since desktop computers are inexpensive now—under $1000, every church should own one.)

Fourth, churches can systematically monitor the performance of local private charities. They can then recommend that families support the well-run ones. The charity that submits to careful scrutiny and passes the test can be put on a list of recommended charities. Members would rely on the deacons to make such investigations. It is a simple matter of good stewardship.

Fifth, churches can mobilize and utilize existing resources within the community networking businesses, service groups, and civic coalitions. For example, the deacons can set up and maintain an employment placement service that would benefit both local businesses and the poor. Or, they can approach landlords with low occupancy rates in their apartment complexes, proposing to place poor families in those units in exchange for mowing the lawns, cleaning the grounds, and light maintenance work.

God's authority must be upheld and the authority of His Word must be established. The church serves as a judge. He who pays the piper calls the tune. He who feeds the piper orders the meal. If someone is under the table of the Lord begging for crumbs, he had better understand just why he is under the table, and just how risky it is to receive scraps from God's table. Paul warned all such dependent sinners about the risk of remaining under the table and refusing God's saving grace:

> Beloved, do not avenge yourselves, but rather give place to wrath; for it is written, "Vengeance is Mine, I will repay," says the Lord. "Therefore if your enemy hungers, feed him; If he thirsts, give him a drink; For in so doing you will heap coals of fire on his head" (Romans 12:19–20).

Conclusion

The church is to do the work of charity, but the modern church has not yet shown itself *capable* of doing it. Paralyzed by theologies of escapism, pessimism, and experientialism, the church lost its position of influence in society and saw humanism take its place.

And charity was thus yielded over to bureaucracies and governments.

In order for the church to regain its place, in order for it to actually *do* the work of charity, providing answers, alternatives, and models, it must *return* to the *Word*. She must return to the Word revealed, the Word incarnate, and the Word made manifest.

The church also needs to understand the basic principle of *dominion through service*. It also needs to recover a full understanding of just what the Bible demands—from families, civil governments, and churches. It must restore the proper use and teaching of the Sacraments, and it must train families to exercise charity. It must stand as the protector of the families of church members. It must not assume more responsibility than is proper, and therefore it must limit its charitable giving, for it is not to accumulate unwarranted power. Power flows to those who exercise responsibility, as the creators and defenders of the messianic state understand so well.

Above all, the church must use its teaching ministry to challenge the moral and economic foundations of modern humanism, which in turn undergirds socialism. The messianic state must be challenged from the moral high ground before it attempts to weaken the church by replacing the church's welfare functions and the welfare functions of families.

Summary

Due to passive and inadequate theologies within the church, Western civilization is facing a series of grave crises that threaten to destroy everything that we hold near and dear.

The enemies of the Gospel have been able to gain control of our culture simply because the church has abandoned the Word—the Word revealed, the Word incarnate, and the Word made manifest.

The central agenda of the church then for the days ahead is simple: Return to the Word.

When the church adheres to the Word she can help the poor in ways no other institution—public or private—possibly can: she renews men's minds, she readjusts them to reality, and she reforms their life styles.

Thus, the church must reassert her proper place in society: mobilizing deacons, instructing families, discipling sinners, encouraging other churches, establishing shelters, etc.

The transformation of our society depends on the faithfulness of the church in this critical matter.

13

WHAT FAMILIES SHOULD DO

Jesus said, "If you love Me, keep my commandments" (John 14:15). And again, "He who has My commandments and keeps them, it is he who loves Me. And he who loves Me will be loved by My Father, and I will love him and manifest Myself to him" (John 14:21).

Similarly, the Apostle John wrote,

Now by this we know that we know Him, if we keep His commandments. He who says, "I know Him," and does not keep His commandments, is a liar, and the truth is not in him. But whoever keeps His word, truly the love of God is perfected in him. By this we know that we are in Him. He who says he abides in Him ought himself also to walk just as He walked. Beloved, I write no new commandment to you, but an old commandment which you have had from the beginning. The old commandment is the word which you heard from the beginning (1 John 2:3–7).

The unmistakable mark of a faithful people is obedience. Believers are proved as "doers of the word, and not hearers only, deceiving yourselves" (James 1:22). They keep the commands of God's Word.

Thus James could ask,

What does it profit, my brethren, if someone says he has faith, but does not have works? Can faith save him? If a brother or sister is naked and destitute of daily food, and one of you says to them, "Depart in peace, be warmed and be filled," but you do not give them the things which are needed for the body, what does it profit? Thus also faith by itself, if it does not have works, is dead. But someone will say, "You have faith, and I have works. Show me your faith without your works, and I will show you my faith by my works" (James 2:14–18).

Regardless of what the government does, regardless even of what the church does, families and individuals have a responsibility to obey God. Every believer has an irrevocable duty to demonstrate the authenticity of their faith. Each of us is called to keep Christ's commandment to show compassion and care for the hurting and for the needy. And each of us is called to lead our family to such service.

There is simply no getting around it. We can make excuses all day long, but they won't change the fact that *we* are obligated by our faith in the Lord Jesus to *do right*. Our federal bureaucracy may be mired in unjust and unfair patterns of welfare oppression, our deacons may utterly ignore their calling in favor of administrative trivialities, and our churches may be sidetracked by theological side issues or evangelical sideshows, but *we* still have no "outs." We have a job to do. We *must* "keep His commandments."

But our obedience must not simply be a dry, lifeless compliance to the letter of the Law. Our righteousness must surpass that of the scribes and the Pharisees (Matthew 5:20). Our righteousness must be marked by *love*. Our obedience is to be a joyous exercise of loving-kindness (Psalm 109:16).

Just as our obedience is evidence that our love for *God is* authentic, so our love for *man is* evidence that our *obedience is* authentic.

Once again, the Apostle of obedience *and* love, John, asserts,

> We know that we have passed from death to life, because we love the brethren. He who does not love his brother abides in death (1 John 3:14).

And again he says,

> By this we know love, because He laid down His life for us. And we also ought to lay down our lives for the brethren. But whoever has this world's goods, and sees his brother in need, and shuts up his heart from him, how does the love of God abide in him? My little children, let us not love in word or in tongue, but in deed and in truth. And by this we know that we are of the truth, and shall assure our heart before Him (1 John 3:1–19).

When asked by the scribes, "What commandment is the foremost of all?" Jesus answered,

> The first of all the commandments is, "Hear, O Israel, the Lord our God, the Lord is one. And you shall love the Lord your God with all your heart, with all your soul, with all your mind, and with all your strength." This is the first commandment. And the second, like it, is this, "You shall love your neighbor as yourself."

There is no other commandment greater than these (Mark 12:29–31).

Our love of God is shown by obedience. Our obedience is shown by love of man. It is an endless cycle. It is a marvelous cycle that makes faith in Christ not just right, and not just true, but abundantly satisfying as well (John 10:7–18).

The Love Connection

"Love" is an overused, much abused word in our everyday vocabularies. When we say that we "love" Mom, hot dogs, apple pie, and baseball, we reduce the word's impact terribly. When "love" can mean one thing to a Hollywood starlet, another to a Madison Avenue ad man, another to a gay activist on Castro Street in San Francisco, another to an Arab terrorist for Qaddafi, and still another to the man on the street in Tulsa, Oklahoma, "love" ceases to mean much at all. In fact, a word that can mean almost anything to anybody will soon come to mean almost nothing to everybody. But, even though our culture may be a bit muddy in its understanding of "love," the Bible is absolutely clear.

> Love suffers long and is kind; love does not envy; love does not parade itself, is not puffed up; does not behave rudely, does not seek its own, is not provoked; thinks no evil; does not rejoice in iniquity, but rejoices in the truth; bears all things, believes all things, hopes all things, endures all things. Love never fails. But whether there are prophecies, they will fail; whether there are tongues, they will cease; whether there is knowledge, it will vanish away (1 Corinthians 13:4–8).

Love involves "compassion, kindness, humility, gentleness, and patience" (Colossians 3:12–14). It involves singlemindedness (Philippians 2:2). It involves purity of heart, a good conscience, and "a faith unfeigned" (1 Timothy 1:5). It involves diligence (2 Corinthians 8:7), knowledge (Philippians 1:9), service (Galatians 5:13), righteousness (2 Timothy 2:22), sound judgement (Philippians 1:9), and courtesy (1 Peter 3:8). Love is the royal Law (James 2:8). It is the capstone of Godly character (1 Corinthians 13:13). It is the message that we have heard from the beginning (1 John 3:11).

Interestingly, the word that the King James translators chose to use in each of these passages was "charity." That word catches a special dynamic of meaning that "love" has lost in our day of muddy definitions. "Charity" accurately communicates the *fact* that love is not simply a feeling. Love is something you *do*. Love is an *action.* Love is a *commitment,* and an *obligation, and a responsibility.* Love is *charity.*

Thus, we are to *prove* "the sincerity of love" (2 Corinthians 8:8), and we are to do it by following "after charity" (1 Corinthians 14:1), by having "fervent charity" among ourselves (1 Peter 4:8), and by being an example to others "in charity" (1 Timothy 4:12). For "charity shall cover a multitude of sins" (1 Peter 4:8).

Though I speak with the tongues of men and of angels, and have not charity, I am become as sounding brass, or a tinkling cymbal. And though I have the gift of prophecy, and understand all mysteries, and all knowledge; and though I have all faith, so that I could remove mountains, and have not charity, I am nothing. And though I bestow all goods to feed the poor, and though I give my body to be burned, and have not charity, it profiteth me nothing (1 Corinthians 13:1–3 KJV).

There is simply no getting around it.

It is a Christian *necessity* to do the work of charity, to love not just "in word or in tongue, but in deed and in truth" (1 John 3:18).

Even if no one else cares. Even if no one else helps. Even if no one else tries. We *must.* Our families *must.*

Encouraging Others

But, wait ...

Just because *right now* you're the only one you know concerned about the plight of the poor doesn't mean that the situation will *always* be that lonely!

As Christians we are to "consider one another in order to stir up love and good works" (Hebrews 10:24).

We are to *encourage* those we know to live lives of love, charity, and compassion (Hebrews 10:25). We should encourage each other by example (1 Timothy 4:12), by intercession (Philippians 1:9), by correspondence (Philippians 2:2), by exhortation (Galatians 5:13), and by entreaty (2 John 5).

We can encourage our pastor, elders, and deacons to study the Scriptures and to deal with the crisis at hand. We can relieve their burdens, protect their time, and enhance their ministry so that they can *do* what God has *called* them to do. We can give them books, and tapes, and pamphlets. We can share with them our ideas, offer them our service, and give them our friendship. We can, in short, *encourage* them.

Charity ultimately can't work, as conceived in Scripture, if only a few isolated individuals, families, and churches participate. But ...

charity *can* get *started* with only a few isolated individuals, families, and churches. (Again, step-by-step procedures, examples, and ideas on *how* to get started may be found in my book, *Bringing in the Sheaves: Transforming Poverty into Productivity,* from Standfast Books).

Those few isolated individuals, families, and churches *can* make a difference. A *big* difference.

But only if they are willing, no matter what, to show their unwavering allegiance to Christ by "keeping His commandments."

A Commitment for the Future

So then, in practical terms, what does this really mean?

What can we *do*?

What can our families do?

First, each of our families can seek ways to help the poor in an immediate, tangible way. Now. We can open our homes to shelter battered children or women in the midst of a crisis pregnancy. We can start a food pantry at the church. On our own. Of our own initiative. We can "adopt" another family in the church or local community that is struggling. We can volunteer part time to work with a Biblical charity ministry in our town, or to work in a crisis pregnancy center, or in a home for abused wives. We can utilize alms giving and our tithe to extend the reach of our family and the church to the hurting and the dispossessed. We can plant a garden, donating the harvest to a foodbank. We can assemble holiday food baskets, teach a Sunday School class on charity, organize a youth missions project, or disciple a young husband or wife on proper stewardship. We can do *something*.

Second, each of our families can utilize its gifts and its influence within the church to encourage a higher profile for Godly deeds of charity. We can encourage, support, and inform our leaders. We can facilitate *their* outreaches. We can open doors of compassion by opening eyes of awareness. We can do *something*.

Third, each of our families can work to coordinate community-wide participation in charity projects. We can work with other pastors, deacons, church benevolence groups, and even other families to build a network of care in our neighborhoods. We can initiate city-wide programs. We can stimulate media interest. We can hold informative meetings, press conferences, and seminars. We can invite guest lecturers. We can establish task forces and community coalitions. We can do *something*.

Fourth, each of our families can knit providence, thrift, and compassion into the fabric of our life together so that we will never fall into the trap of poverty ourselves. We can teach our children financial and resource management through the use of basic Biblical strategies like budgeting (Luke 14, 16), saving (Proverbs 6), setting goals (Proverbs 1), investment (Matthew 21), the eradication of debt (Romans 13:8), and of course the tithe (Malachi 3:8–12). We can teach them proper standards of physical health through regular hygiene (Leviticus 15; Numbers 19; Deuteronomy 23), exercise (1 Corinthians 6:18–21; 3 John 2), nutrition (Leviticus 7:22; Deuteronomy 32:14–15), and rest (Exodus 20:8–10; Psalm 23; Hebrews 4; Mark 6:31–32). We can nurture in them literacy and education, building Godly character through discipline and learning (Deuteronomy 4:9, 6:6–8; 2 Timothy 4:13; Proverbs 3:1–12). We can help them develop future or alternate careers through family businesses, entrepreneurial projects, and learning a secondary trade. We can provide social, emotional, and spiritual strength by spending quality time with them (1 Samuel 7–8; Leviticus 23:40–43), by utilizing our leisure hours wisely (Ecclesiastes 11:9–10; Proverbs 8:30–31), and by exercising strict discipline (1 Kings 1:6; Proverbs 22:6, 22:25). We can even begin a program of home production and storage, providing for our family contingency plans in times of emergencies (Proverbs 29:18; Luke 12:48, 16:11; Genesis 41). We can do something.

Certainly there is no lack of places to start.

So what is holding us back? Why do we hesitate?

A new commandment I give to you, that you love one another; as I have loved you, that you also love one another (John 13:34).

Therefore, pursue charity (1 Corinthians 14:1), to prove the sincerity of your love (2 Corinthians 8:7).

Conclusion

Love is something you do, not just something you feel. This truth is underlined in Scripture time after time. And this love, this active love, this charitable love, then becomes evidence that we really do love Christ. We obey His commandments, but we obey in the context of love.

This is the bottom line.

So, it doesn't really matter what the government does or doesn't do; we have a responsibility to do our job. To love and to obey.

That means that we need to go to work. We need to mobilize our families. We need to take the Biblical *principles* for welfare and hammer them into practical strategies for charity.

But, we don't have to do that all alone. We can encourage. We can coordinate. We can lay the foundations. We can do something. We can.

And we must.

After all, there is starving in the shadow of plenty.

Summary

Regardless of what the government does, regardless of what the church does, families and individuals have a responsibility to obey God.

Since charity is primarily a function of the Christian family working in concert with other Christian families, it is essential that each of those Christian families begin to implement the love of God practically, tangibly, and forthrightly.

Charity begins at home: educating children, caring for the helpless, and shoring up the weak. It begins as we encourage others, coordinate resources, network with existing programs, and spearhead new efforts.

Something *can* be done. So, something *must* be done. After all, there is starving in the shadow of plenty.

FOR FURTHER READING

David Chilton, *Productive Christians in an Age of Guilt-Manipulators,* (Tyler, Texas: Institute for Christian Economics, 1981; 3rd edition, 1985).

Gary DeMar, *God and Government: A Biblical and Historical Study,* (Atlanta, Georgia: American Vision Press, 1982).

_____. *God and Government: Issues in Biblical Perspective,* (Atlanta, Georgia: American Vision Press, 1984).

_____. *God and Government: The Restoration of the Republic,* (Atlanta, Georgia: American Vision Press, 1986).

George Gilder, *Wealth and Poverty,* (New York, New York: Basic Books, 1981).

George Grant, *Bringing in the Sheaves: Transforming Poverty into Productivity,* (1985).

_____. *The Dispossessed: Homelessness in America,* (Fort Worth, Texas: Dominion Press, 1986).

James B. Jordan, *The Sociology of the Church,* (Tyler, Texas: Geneva Ministries, 1986).

Lawrence Mead, *Beyond Entitlement: The Social Obligations of Citizenship,* (New York, New York: The Free Press, 1986).

Charles Murray, *Losing Ground: American Social Policy 1950–1980,* (New York, New York: Basic Books, 1984).

Gary North, *The Sinai Strategy: Economics and the Ten Commandments,* (Tyler, Texas: Institute for Christian Economics, 1986).

_____. *Unholy Spirits: Occultism and New Age Humanism,* (Fort Worth: Dominion Press, 1986).

_____. *An Introduction to Christian Economics,* (Nutley, New Jersey: Craig Press, 1973).

R. J. Rushdoony, *The Institutes of Biblical Law,* (Phillipsburg, New Jersey: Presbyterian and Reformed Publishing Company, 1973).

Herbert Schlossberg, *Idols for Destruction,* (Nashville, Tennessee: Thomas Nelson Publishers, 1983).

Ray Sutton, *That You May Prosper: Dominion by Covenant.* (Fort Worth, Texas, Dominion Press, 1986).

Thomas Sowell, *Civil Rights: Rhetoric or Reality?,* (New York, New York: William Morrow and Company, 1983).

Walter Williams, *The State Against Blacks,* (New York, New York: McGraw Hill Book Company, 1982).

SUBJECT INDEX

Build Your Christian School Curriculum
with DISCOUNT BOOKS
from *Christian Liberty Press*